'This excellent and varied chaplaincy studies' place a public theology. In affirming the mission of God as beginning in the world beyond the church, it challenges us, in turn, to become a more worldly church through the practices of discernment, participation and witness.'

– Elaine Graham, Grosvenor Professor of Practical Theology, University of Chester

'With the massive changes currently going on in the public sector, churches, along with our colleagues in the voluntary sector, are being looked to as partners in ways we have not known for decades. In chaplaincy, we have models to help us do this effectively but, all too often, a lack of theological reflection on its guiding principles leaves us diminished. These essays help to fill that gap and I warmly commend them.'

– The Right Reverend Colin Fletcher, Bishop of Dorchester

'Chaplaincy is flourishing in the twenty-first century, and one of its great needs is for a Christian wisdom that can open up its depths and potential and also face its challenges. This book meets that need. It offers helpful ideas, models, images and experiences to think with, and it has the capacity to inspire ministries of meaning and practical action in diverse settings of our complex society.'

– David F. Ford, OBE, Regius Professor of Divinity Emeritus, University of Cambridge

A CHRISTIAN THEOLOGY OF CHAPLAINCY

Edited by John Caperon, Andrew Todd and James Walters

Foreword by Martin Seeley

Jessica Kingsley *Publishers*
London and Philadelphia

First published in 2018
by Jessica Kingsley Publishers
73 Collier Street
London N1 9BE, UK
and
400 Market Street, Suite 400
Philadelphia, PA 19106, USA

www.jkp.com

Library of Congress Cataloging in Publication Data
Names: Caperon, John, 1944- editor.
Title: A Christian Theology of Chaplaincy / edited by John Caperon, Andrew
Todd, and James Walters.
Description: Philadelphia : Jessica Kingsley Publishers, 2017. | Description
based on print version record and CIP data provided by publisher.
Identifiers: LCCN 2017012835 (print) | LCCN 2017030605 (ebook) | ISBN
9781784503536 (e-book) | ISBN 9781785920905 (alk. paper)
Subjects: LCSH: Chaplains. | Pastoral theology. | Theology.
Classification: LCC BV4375 (ebook) | LCC BV4375 .C53 2017 (print) | DDC
253--dc23

British Library Cataloguing in Publication Data
A CIP catalogue record for this book is available from the British Library

ISBN 978 1 78592 090 5
eISBN 978 1 78450 353 6

CONTENTS

FOREWORD
MARTIN SEELEY

The evident reality is that most chaplains spend the vast majority of their time with people who are not Christians. Many chaplains have no sacred building or space to be identified with or based at. Their apostolic ministry is to be placed deeply in the world, to witness to the work of the Spirit in the countless places of God's interweaving, of God's leavening. Chaplains embody the gospel, and the manner of their being changes lives.

All Christian disciples are called to be in these places, at these intersections of Church and world, of faith and society, but chaplains are a particular, powerful and public manifestation of this gifted presence.

This book began life as a symposium at Westcott House, Cambridge, held in April 2015, drawing together lay and ordained chaplains from schools, higher education, healthcare, the police, the military and business to tease out the theological, missiological and ecclesiological questions that chaplaincy is currently bringing into sharp focus.

Behind this interrogative engagement lay the puzzling question: why, when chaplaincy seems to be proliferating in an increasing diversity of contexts, and the Church is simultaneously recognising its critical need to be actively present in communities where the gospel is hardly known, why is chaplaincy so little valued as an essential – or *the* essential – part of the Church's response to God's call to be actively present for the world?

Is that because it doesn't 'count' in the Church's sums? It would be interesting to see what happened to chaplaincy if dioceses were to include in their statistics chaplain-led acts of worship in schools, military bases and healthcare institutions.

Is it because sustaining chaplaincy is often largely out of the hands of the Church structures?

Is it because chaplaincy often exists on the ecumenical and interfaith intersections, placing it, as one author here describes, in an apophatic rather than a doctrinal position?

The thread that runs through this book is the quality of transforming presence that chaplaincy embodies. That transforming presence is rooted in the chaplain's attentiveness to God's presence and activity in contexts that we may otherwise ignore or of which we are unaware. As one author expresses it, chaplains stand in the world, looking around, creatively responding to what they see.

This ministry requires particular gifts, including attending to, listening to and interpreting God's activity in the lives of individuals and institutions. It is about enabling people to live the fullness of their humanity, and, as another author writes, creating 'transformational encounters' for people.

Chaplains are required to be bilingual, and to carry this skill with them without relying on the prompts of ritual and place. Like all public ministries, it can be lonely and the seduction to over-identify with the context being served is always high. But it is a highly creative ministry, requiring an agile faithfulness and pastoral imagination.

I hope this book contributes to the Church's growing realisation that chaplaincy is an agent of transformation where the Church otherwise is not, that chaplaincy is a vital agent of renewal – for the world.

The Rt Revd Martin Seeley
Bishop of St Edmundsbury and Ipswich
Chair of the Church of England's Ministry Council

LIST OF CONTRIBUTORS

The Revd Charlotte Bradley has been Chaplain & Interfaith Advisor to University College London (UCL) since 2013 and is Honorary Associate Priest at St Pancras Church, in whose parish UCL lies. She studied theology at Pembroke College, Oxford, and trained for ordination at Westcott House, Cambridge, where she completed an MPhil in Church History. She served her curacy in the Parish of Chipping Barnet in St Albans Diocese before taking up her present post. In 2016, alongside the Revd Dr James Walters, she co-founded The Anchorage, a new worshipping community for university students in London, which meets on Sunday evenings in a university building. She also works on young vocations initiatives in the Diocese of London.

The Revd Dr John Caperon is a parish priest on the Ashdown Forest, East Sussex. Ordained in 1984 as a non-stipendiary priest, he worked as an English teacher and headteacher in secondary schools, and subsequently as a consultant and trainer for the Association of School and College Leaders. From 2006–11 he was Director of the Bloxham Project working in support of school chaplaincy. Having undertaken the first empirical research into school chaplaincy in Church schools in England through the Cambridge Theological Federation, he was awarded his doctorate in Practical Theology in 2013. His book, *A Vital Ministry: Chaplaincy in Schools in the Post-Christian Era,* was published by SCM Press in 2015.

Ben Ryan is a researcher at the Christian thinktank Theos. He holds degrees in Theology and Religious Studies from the University of Cambridge and in European Studies from the London School of Economics. He is the author of a number of Theos reports, including *A Very Modern Ministry: Chaplaincy in the UK* (2015) and *Catholic Social Thought and Catholic Charities in Britain Today: Need and Opportunity* (2016).

The Revd Canon Dr Andrew Todd is Programme Leader in Christian Spirituality and Co-ordinator for the Centre for Contemporary Spirituality at Sarum College, Salisbury. From 2006 to early 2017 he was Director of the Cardiff Centre for Chaplaincy Studies. During that time, he published widely on chaplaincy and related issues. His publications include: Chris Swift, Mark Cobb and Andrew Todd (eds), *A Handbook of Chaplaincy Studies* (2015); Jonathan Pye, Peter Sedgwick and Andrew Todd (eds), *Critical Care: Delivering Spiritual Care in Healthcare Contexts* (2015); Andrew Todd (ed.), *Military Chaplaincy in Contention: Chaplains, Churches, and the Morality of Conflict* (2013). He is a practical theologian and ethnographer, with particular interests in contemporary religion and spirituality, and their interaction with longer established faith traditions. He is an Honorary Research Fellow of Cardiff University and a past President of the Cambridge Theological Federation.

The Revd Canon Dr James Walters is chaplain at the London School of Economics (LSE). He is a senior lecturer in practice at the LSE Marshall Institute of Philanthropy and a senior fellow of the LSE Institute of Public Affairs. He is also Founder and Director of the LSE Faith Centre, which seeks to promote religious literacy and develop interfaith leadership among the university's diverse student body. Dr Walters writes on philosophy, politics and theology and published his study of the French philosopher Jean Baudrillard with Bloomsbury in 2012. He is also co-leader of The Anchorage, a new worshipping community for students in London, launched in 2016.

The Revd Canon Dr Margaret Whipp is the lead chaplain for the Oxford University Hospitals. Her first profession was in medicine. Since ordination she has served in parish ministry, university chaplaincy, and more recently as Senior Tutor at Ripon College Cuddesdon. She writes and researches in pastoral theology, enjoys singing and long-distance pilgrimage trails, and serves as the Catechist for Exeter College, Oxford. She is the author of the *SCM Studyguide in Pastoral Theology* (2013) and is a regular contributor to the series of Reflections for Daily Prayer (Church House Publishing). Her book, *Graceful Waiting*, will be released in 2017 by Canterbury Press. She is an Honorary Canon of Christchurch Cathedral, Oxford.

The Revd Dr Rowan Clare Williams has been Anglican chaplain to the University of York since 2010. She was formerly chaplain to Leicester Royal Infirmary, working in a multi-faith team, and has a professional background in residential healthcare. Her publications include *A Condition of Complete Simplicity* (2003) and *Singing in a Strange Land: A Theology of Chaplaincy from a Higher Education Perspective*, to be published by Grove Books in summer 2017.

INTRODUCTION

The Age of Chaplaincy?

JOHN CAPERON

The situation of institutional religion in Britain in the early twenty-first century is complex, even confusing. At a time when church attendance in the established denominations is continuing to decline to lower levels than ever recorded, there is an upsurge in the membership of black Pentecostal church communities (Sherwood 2016) and a sense that older, traditional versions of Christian faith may be giving way to newer expressions (Torres 2016). At the same time, there may be a move towards 'spirituality' rather than 'religion', in the 'spiritual revolution' described by researchers into religious practice in one English small town (Heelas and Woodhead 2005). It may even be that religion in Britain is moving towards a period remarkably different from its past: one sociologist of religion provocatively suggests that the future of religion in Britain is 'brown and black', to be found not in traditional Christianity at all, but in Islam and the black majority churches (Voas 2015).

Whatever the future holds, there is little doubt about the present situation. Perhaps the most devastating analysis of the current religious context has been that by Linda Woodhead, whose own survey work, combined with data from the 2011 Census and the British Social Attitudes Survey, has led to conclusions set out in her British Academy Lecture, 'The rise of "no religion" in Britain: the emergence of a new cultural majority'. Woodhead demonstrates compellingly that there is now a majority of British adults who describe themselves as having 'no religion'. These 'nones', as she terms them, are a new cultural majority, and the explanation for this situation lies not only in cultural pluralisation and ethical liberalisation, but in what she sees as 'the opposite direction of travel' of the churches, with the question of same-sex marriage being a crucial indicator. In a book co-written with the journalist Andrew Brown, Woodhead further develops this argument, that the Church of England, in particular, has lost its cultural influence as a result of the 'ethical gap' between an increasingly liberalised population and a backward-looking Church; this she argues is precisely how 'the Church of England lost the English people' (Brown and Woodhead 2016). The outcome is, says Woodhead, that Britain is now most accurately described as 'between Christian and "no religion"' (Woodhead 2016).

The response of the British churches to their increasing marginalisation in society has been varied. In the Church of England, the main institutional response since 2015 has been the Renewal and Reform initiative, under which halting the decline in numbers and achieving church growth has been the key objective, together with an emphasis on recruiting more ordinands and supporting related new initiatives such as church planting. This has brought a renewed emphasis on evangelisation, on personal discipleship and the role of church members in spreading the faith, a direction of travel that has won most support from those of evangelical sympathy within the Church. On a wider front, recent studies appear to show that within the worldwide Anglican communion there is a mixed picture of growth and decline, with the size of the communion having, it is estimated, doubled in the past 50 years, most of this growth being in the global South. One observer notes the danger of churches in the global North adopting a 'decline theology' which sees decline as unproblematic and even inevitable, leading to an 'ecclesiology of fatalism' (Goodhew 2017). Clearly, the

Church of England at national leadership level has shunned this direction and determined instead to counteract decline; though what will actually happen in the various dioceses and parishes of the land is as yet uncertain.

While all this has been happening, another and apparently unrelated development has occurred, namely an unplanned but vigorous burgeoning of the ministry of chaplaincy. The first evidence of the extent of chaplaincy in the Church of England context emerged in a report to the Church's Mission and Public Affairs division in 2014 (Todd *et al.* 2014). Remarkably, the Church had previously possessed no clear factual basis for reckoning how many clergy and others were involved in chaplaincy ministry, and the report's conclusion, that a minimum of 1415 reported chaplains were known to the Church of England, was therefore startling. The further conclusion, that this minimum figure was a 'significant underestimate, especially in relation to the scale of lay volunteers involved in chaplaincy' (p.7), gave some indication of what might be the real extent of chaplaincy.

That extent was explored in an important case study undertaken by Ben Ryan for Theos (Ryan 2015). Researching chaplaincy in the mixed-community town of Luton, Ryan demonstrated that Luton's nine different chaplaincy providers were sending 'an astonishing total' of 169 chaplains to support the local community. Given a population of some quarter of a million, that means one chaplain for something under 1500 people – a rather better ratio than the churches can offer in the traditional sphere of parish ministry. The Theos study does come with caveats, however. Ryan is clear that there is 'very little consensus' among chaplaincy providers about how to define what a chaplain is. In effect, his research accepts a self-defining understanding of chaplaincy, covering both traditional, statutory chaplaincy spheres such as prison chaplaincy; non-statutory but long-established spheres such as education; and chaplaincy in a new range of other community contexts (see also Slater 2015). Moreover, the term 'chaplain' covers both those working full-time, 'embedded' within institutions, as well as those visiting institutions from outside. Ryan's broad, adopted definition of a chaplain is 'an individual who provides religious and spiritual care within an organisational setting' (Ryan 2015, p.10).

What does this apparent burgeoning of chaplaincy provision mean? At one level, it seems to be a response of the churches and other religious groups to perceived personal and pastoral need within the community. It is as if providers, conscious of a pastoral deficit existing despite the churches' traditional ministerial activities, are seeking to offer additional or alternative provision of care. What might cause concern is that in this apparent explosion of chaplaincy provision, there is no agreed understanding of what a chaplain is; who counts as a chaplain; what qualities or qualifications a chaplain might have; what a chaplain's accountability might be to sponsoring organisation or to clients; or indeed what a chaplain's motivation and intention might be.

At another level, the growth of chaplaincy can be seen as a response to the decline in church attendance, the increasing marginalisation of the churches, and their remoteness from everyday life as experienced by the overwhelming majority of people. If this is so, it is remarkable that it is apparently occurring largely without any deliberate, strategic intention on the part of the churches, but simply growing, Topsy-like. As far as the Church of England – the home of traditional and statutory chaplaincies – is concerned, there has simply been no declared intention in relation to chaplaincy. The Church's traditional provision of pastoral ministry has been through the parish system and the parish priest, or vicar. Furthermore, Church of England chaplains report a sense of their own marginality in relation to the Church: here is a ministerial sphere that has been largely unrecognised and unsupported by the Church. The Church's intentionality appears largely limited to its future involvement in the traditional pattern of priest and parish.

In this context, it is perhaps unsurprising that there is a serious theological deficit in relation to chaplaincy. Available book-size resources are limited. Giles Legood's *Chaplaincy: The Church's Sector Ministries* (1999) offered a significant essay by Paul Avis placing chaplaincy in the context of the Church's mission and ministry, but most of the volume was taken up with narrative-style accounts of different chaplaincy spheres. In addition, it was scarcely helpful that the book's title used the term 'sector ministries': this could almost have been designed to demonstrate the Church's institutional view of the partial, incomplete nature of the ministry of chaplaincy, by implied comparison with the traditional, holistic ministry of parish priests. *Being a Chaplain* (Threlfall-Holmes and Newett 2011) was again largely based on the narratives of chaplains in varying situations, but also offered a series of thoughtful theological reflections on the nature of chaplaincy and its place within the 'mixed economy' of different modes of ministry. But there remains a theological deficit; and what this book seeks to do is to begin to remedy that deficit.

Originating from a theological symposium gathered at Westcott House, Cambridge, by its then Principal Dr Martin Seeley in 2015, this book offers a series of chapters which together form a theological exploration of chaplaincy. The standpoint of the authors is largely Anglican: all with the exception of Ben Ryan are Church of England priests, and all are working or have worked as chaplains. For all the authors, the underlying question could be framed as: what is the meaning of chaplaincy as a ministry of the Church, and what is its distinctiveness in contributing to the mission of the Church in the twenty-first century?

The first chapter, by Andrew Todd, develops a fundamental theology of the world, an understanding rooted in incarnational thought and highlighting the Christological identity of humanity. In his chapter on ecclesiology, James Walters explores the locus of chaplaincy, inhabiting the intersection of Church and world, while in her chapter on the multi-faith context, experienced sharply in higher education chaplaincy, Rowan Williams argues for an orthodox theological basis for multi-faith engagement. Ben Ryan examines critically the various models of chaplaincy available to us, and focuses on the potential of chaplaincy to create transformational human encounters. In her chapter, Margaret Whipp explores from a healthcare perspective the nature and integrity of embedded chaplaincy, and the significance of the chaplain's presence. John Caperon's chapter reflects on the Church of England's traditional pattern of ministry, and identifies chaplaincy as both overlooked by the institutional Church and yet having the potential in its pastoral focus to be a key ministerial paradigm in the present century. James Walters and Charlotte Bradley look at what the Church of England's current evangelistic imperative can mean in a secular higher education institution, arguing for clear integrity of purpose. And in the concluding chapter, Andrew Todd invites us, in the light of a non-institutional understanding of 'religion', to re-envisage theology itself, arguing that chaplaincy points towards a theology, or theologies, that can do justice both to the breadth of chaplains' own experience of religion and to the full extent of divine presence and action in the world. What together the authors have attempted is simply a beginning – an invitation to further practical theological reflection rooted in and prompted by chaplaincy.

References

Brown, A. and Woodhead, L. (2016) *That Was the Church That Was: How the Church of England Lost the English People.* London and New York: Bloomsbury.

Goodhew, D. (2017) 'A story of growth and decline.' *Church Times.* Accessed on 7/7/2017 at: www.churchtimes.co.uk/articles/2017/6-january/features/features/a-story-of-growth-and-decline#.

Heelas, P. and Woodhead, L. (2005) *The Spiritual Revolution: Why Religion is Giving Way to Spirituality.* Malden MA; Oxford, Carlton Victoria: Blackwell.

Legood, G. (ed.) (1999) *Chaplaincy: The Church's Sector Ministries.* London and New York: Cassell.

Ryan, B. (2015) *A Very Modern Ministry: Chaplaincy in the UK.* London: Theos.

Sherwood, H. (2016) 'Pentecostal church looks to white Britons to boost congregations.' *The Guardian.* London, Guardian Media. Accessed on 7/7/2017 at: www.theguardian.com/world/2016/dec/30/pentecostal-church-looks-to-white-britons-to-boost-congregations.

Slater, V. (2015) *Chaplaincy Ministry and the Church of England.* London: SCM Press.

Threlfall-Holmes, M. and Newett, M. (2011) *Being a Chaplain.* London: SPCK.

Todd, A. *et al.* (2014) 'The Church of England's Involvement in Chaplaincy.' Cardiff & Cuddesdon: Cardiff Centre for Chaplaincy Studies and Oxford Centre for Ecclesiology and Practical Theology. Accessed on 7/7/2017 at: http://stmichaels. ac.uk/assets/pdf/Todd__Slater___Dunlop_2014_Report_on_Church_of_ England_Chaplaincy.pdf.

Torres, H. (2016) 'Christianity in UK sees seismic shift.' *Christianity Today.* Accessed on 7/7/17 at: www.christiantoday.com/article/christianity.in.u.k.sees. seismic.shift.as.pentecostal.and.charismatic.churches.thrive.replacing.aging. churches/83054.htm.

Voas, D. (2015) 'What is the future for religion in Britain?' Theos. Accessed on 7/7/2017 at: www.theosthinktank.co.uk/comment/2015/02/02/what-is-the-future-for-religion-in-britain.

Woodhead, L. (2016) 'The rise of "no religion" in Britain: the emergence of a new cultural majority.' *Journal of the British Academy (4):* 245–61. Accessed on 7/7/2017 at: www.britac.ac.uk/sites/default/files/11%20Woodhead%201825.pdf.

1

A THEOLOGY OF THE WORLD

— ANDREW TODD —

Introduction

Chaplaincy functions characteristically in the 'world', rather than in relation to the life of the gathered Church. Christian chaplaincy is part of the way in which the Church, through its members, inhabits and serves the 'world', as a living witness to the gospel among people of diverse faiths and beliefs, an embodied engagement with different world views and practices. Christian chaplains serve and live the gospel in different social domains, in workplaces of many different kinds, in criminal justice settings, in healthcare, in the armed forces, in sport and theatre, to name but a few. In living in such domains alongside people, they encounter their values and beliefs, their rituals and ways of being and doing, along with a vast array of social identities and existential questions.

The premise for this chapter is that the engagement of chaplaincy with the presence and action of God in diverse settings and people implies and requires a theology of the world. The chapter will show how this theology needs to address the way in which God's presence and action may be discerned in the lives and actions of people who exhibit a diversity of practice and belief. This is necessary in order to resist an unwarranted dualism in which God's presence and action are perceived as restricted to certain areas of life; to ensure that our theology of God's presence and action extends beyond the life and work of the Church (especially in a post-Christendom context); and to address questions raised by a plural and pluralistic context.

This chapter first identifies some of the dimensions of the diversity of chaplaincy, in order to underline the need for a sufficiently broad and robust theology. It then examines a theology familiar to Christian chaplains, that chaplains incarnate the love and presence of God in their work. It considers the adequacy of this theology for the task identified, drawing on earlier iterations of Anglican incarnational theology, and considers both the potential scope and criticality of such an approach. The result is a new and deeper incarnational theology of chaplaincy. Finally, the chapter considers the implications for a missiological and ecclesiological framework that relocates chaplaincy in relation to the whole Church.

The diversity of chaplaincy

The Theos report on chaplaincy, *A Very Modern Ministry*, indicates the interaction of chaplaincy with 16 fields of social life in Luton (Ryan 2015). It shows that chaplaincy continues in strength in its traditional areas such as the university, hospital and hospice, but in such settings increasingly has multi-faith teams and multi-faith spaces (the latter complementing traditional chapels). Another traditional chaplaincy area, work in schools, is a feature in Luton too, but in state secondary schools, rather than the historic domain of private schools. And chaplaincy in relation to criminal justice is extending from traditional prison ministry to work with ex-offenders in the community and in courts of justice. In other areas of social life, chaplaincy is finding new work in place of old. In place of earlier models of chaplains in industry, Luton reveals (as do other locations) newer models of chaplains in a variety of commercial and retail workplaces, in the airport and town centre, and with the fire and rescue service. One very new setting for a chaplain is the casino. Finally, as well as working in various organisations, chaplaincy exhibits a commitment to a community model, for example in working in the town centre with homeless and other people.

This picture, drawn from an analysis of chaplaincy's presence in one geographical location, is indicative of the demographics of those with whom chaplains engage. It includes particular age groups, such as those in secondary education or at university; particular social groups, such as ex-offenders; dimensions of life which in part define social identity, including health, education and employment; and different cultures and beliefs. This underlines that chaplains as a whole engage with significant social diversity. This is further reinforced by the wider range of social fields touched by chaplaincy, identified through other research in the report (Ryan 2015, pp.14–16).

Against this background, and in response to the increasing diversity of those served by chaplains, chaplaincy has itself become more diverse. This is most obviously seen in the growth of multi-faith chaplaincy, with chaplains of different faiths and denominations working together (see Gilliat-Ray, Ali and Pattison 2013; Todd 2011, 2013a, 2014). This is significant both as a response to a diverse, increasingly globalised, society and as an example of partnership across different cultures and beliefs. However, multi-faith chaplaincy is not the only response to a globalised context. Luton is illustrative of different approaches, including multi-faith chaplaincy in public settings highlighted above; some chaplaincy with a distinctive Christian ethos (including Luton Churches Education Trust and Luton Town Centre Chaplaincy); and some which is sponsored, or initiated by churches, but which works with a firm equal opportunity policy (such as the Community Resettlement Support Project). But the first and last of these do work across differences of culture and belief within the shared practice of chaplaincy, and all kinds of chaplaincy in Luton have some engagement with a globalised society.

Two kinds of critical theological issue emerge from the diversity of chaplaincy indicated above. One kind has to do with the engagement of chaplains with social areas that raise particular critical questions. In Luton, the most striking example would be the presence of a chaplain in a casino – how does a faith practitioner reflect theologically about their presence in the midst of the gambling industry? Elsewhere the question has been raised in relation to armed forces chaplains living and working with those trained to use lethal force when authorised to do so (Todd 2013b).

The other kind of issue is raised by chaplaincy's engagement with different religious beliefs and with the pluralistic context which holds that manifesting religion or belief is a human right and a 'protected characteristic' (Equality Act 2010). This raises questions about how chaplains reflect theologically about different beliefs and about pluralism, which holds that diversity, including diversity of belief, is a public good contributing to the wellbeing of society (Beckford 2003). These issues are sharpened by chaplains working together across boundaries of belief, not least because the theological response to plural beliefs needs also to provide a basis for dialogue within and about, for example, multi-faith teams and spaces.

The fundamental theological question is whether there is any area of social life where God is not present and where God cannot act. The *prima facie* answer to this question must be that God is present and may act in any and every area of social life. Avoidance of dualism requires that there are no 'no-go areas' for God in God's creation. Two secondary, but vital, questions follow. First, how can theology enable the discernment of God's presence, action and will in particular social settings? This appears most important in settings where the critical questions, like those highlighted above, are sharpest, but it is significant in every social setting.

Second, especially, but not exclusively, in situations where chaplains work across boundaries of belief, what sources of theology inform the theological discernment process? The point here is that seeking to be open to the presence and action of God in any situation also implies an openness to reflection on the way God is revealed and, therefore, to all those who seek to reflect in this way. As will be explored further below, this open approach to diverse sources of theology implies a need for dialogue among those engaged in the theological pursuit, whatever their belief tradition.

Incarnational theology

In search of a theological approach that addresses the above questions, one might ask whether any existing contemporary theology of, or inspired by, chaplaincy is sufficiently broad in scope and robust enough in critical engagement to respond to the above questions. A common theological basis for Christian chaplaincy is that chaplains incarnate the presence and love of God (see e.g. Todd, Slater and Dunlop 2014, p.30). This is in keeping with the primary purpose of chaplaincy being seen as pastoral. Sometimes, chaplains will also describe themselves as having a 'prophetic' role, acting as a critical friend to the organisation they serve, perhaps highlighting a failure of the organisation to fully recognise the humanity of an individual or group (see e.g. Torry 2010, pp.187–88). But this role is usually contingent on the 'presence' of the chaplain in the organisation – on their already being embedded in and trusted by the members of that organisation.[1]

The scope of incarnational theology

Given that being 'incarnational' is already a significant way in which chaplains reflect theologically on their embeddedness in social settings, it seems appropriate to explore further both

---

[1]   Clearly, chaplains have used other theologically oriented models, including priest and pastor. The former seems to be less espoused by chaplains (at least in recent research of their views); the latter will be considered later in this chapter.

the scope of this understanding of the incarnational character of chaplaincy and its critical edge. The first evaluative task, therefore, is to discern whether an 'incarnational' theology of chaplaincy is broad enough to enable identification of God's presence and action in diverse social settings. Two things might militate against such a broad application. One is to regard the incarnational work as limited to the person of the chaplain – a clericalisation of this theological approach. While this is a possible narrowing of chaplains' use of incarnation, most Christian chaplains, even if tempted down this track, would quickly recognise and affirm that many in the pastoral situations, which are their daily experience, reveal God's love in action and/or in word. This latter, wider perspective is more likely in contemporary chaplaincy than previously, with the current mixed economy of ordained and lay, employed and volunteer chaplains (see Todd, Slater and Dunlop 2014, pp.19–20, 21–22; Ryan 2015, pp.20–24) than previously. It is also made more likely by those instances of chaplains working together with other Christians in the workplace to reflect theologically on issues and respond appropriately (see Todd, Slater and Dunlop 2014, p.33; Torry 2010).

The breadth of perspective on the range of people in whom we may encounter Christ may also help guard against the second narrowing of an incarnational theology, which is to suggest that an incarnational Christology is only realised in and through the baptised. I would argue that this ecclesiological narrowing is a misreading of the Councils of Nicaea, Constantinople and Chalcedon. Their affirmation of the full humanity of Christ implies that the incarnation of Christ means that humanity, rather than just the Church, has a Christological character. This is a theology, not just an ecclesiology. Therefore, Christ is encountered not only in the person of the chaplain, nor only in the persons of the baptised, but also may be encountered in any human. This is not about making such human persons anonymous Christians, but rather recognising the encounter with them as one with Christ.

Of course, to have a proper breadth, the theology of chaplaincy needs also to be fully Trinitarian, recognising the creating work of the Father and the sustaining work of the Spirit, which are similarly not only to be found in/through the baptised. Thus, for example, wherever, and through whomever, healing or reconciliation are realised, this is the work of the Holy Spirit and of the Godhead.

In terms of reflecting theologically in diverse settings, the above positions encourage the theologian (chaplain or otherwise) to be open to the possibility of discerning God's presence and action in/through any human person involved (as well as through other orders of creation). This is a theology that is broad enough in scope to be applied to any and every social setting. It holds to the principle that God may be present and active in any and every setting. It also recognises as sources of theology not only the reason or experience of the chaplain, or of the baptised, but of any human person in that situation. This theology is in keeping with the open attentiveness of the chaplain in different social settings and situations.

Earlier iterations of incarnational theology

The above theology also builds, to some extent at least, on earlier iterations of incarnational theology, especially with those associated with Anglican social theology rooted in the tradition of Charles Gore and the other contributors to *Lux Mundi*, first published in 1889 (Gore 1904). Thus, for example, Illingworth, in one of his chapters in *Lux Mundi*, seeks to restate the importance of a broad understanding of the incarnation, such that: 'Every creature is a divine word, for it tells of God' (Illingworth 1904, p.135). In this he draws, as in this quotation from Bonaventure, on the patristic and scholastic writers. The purpose of such reflection, however, in the modern period in which Gore *et al.* write, is to engage in a positive theological way with contemporary rational thinking, for example of those who propounded evolutionary theory. Thus in support of this, Illingworth appeals to Aquinas, reiterating his statement that, 'Every intellectual process has its origin in the Word of God Who is the Divine reason' (Illingworth 1904, p.136).

This is an optimistic theology and that optimism may be unwarranted from our contemporary perspective. However, it attempts two things that are of particular relevance to a theology of chaplaincy. It seeks the potential unity of human knowledge, in the face of historic church suspicion of scientific enquiry. In locating scientific and historical intellectual endeavour as aspects of the incarnation of the 'Word of God', Illingworth is suggesting that all human knowledge may contribute to our understanding of humanity or creation, including to our theological knowledge of humanity or creation in relation to God.

The second thing that is attempted is to show that the incarnation is seen in the development of the modern world, and that therefore God is revealed in and through that world. Thus Illingworth again:

> It is true that secular civilisation has co-operated with Christianity to produce the modern world. But secular civilisation is, as we have seen, in the Christian view, nothing less than the providential correlative and counterpart of the incarnation. (Illingworth 1904, p.155)

Michael Ramsey points to the value of this Anglican tradition with the incarnation at its centre:

> It enabled a genuine contact between supernatural religion and contemporary culture. It enabled a meeting-place between revelation and the keen contemporary sense of the importance of historical inquiry. (Ramsey 1960, p.28)

Ramsey is also clear, however, of the pitfalls inherent in such an approach, particularly that:

(i) *explanation* rather than *atonement* can tend to dominate the theological scene, (ii) that *reason* can depress the place and meaning of *faith* in the approach to revealed truth, (iii) that the giving of prominence to this particular dogma can cause other categories of Biblical language and thought to recede from their rightful prominence. (1960, p.27)

Ramsey also provides a helpful reminder that perhaps the last great exponent of this tradition, William Temple, responded late in life (not least in relation to the events of the Second World War) against its optimism, particularly its optimistic aim of offering the incarnation as key to a unifying theory of human experience. As Ramsey puts it:

William Temple, after pursuing a theology of explanation over many of its pitfalls, came to confess that the needs of the hour bade a theology of explanation yield place to a theology of redemption. (1960, p.28; see also pp.159–61)

This chimes with a contemporary perspective on the tradition rooted in *Lux Mundi* that might well hold that it is over optimistic. The events of the twentieth century, both the global and more local conflicts that have characterised that period, and the continued secularisation of our society, make it difficult to fully embrace Illingworth's language. They also might create a theological desire to hold together redemption through knowledge (and a theology of incarnation) with redemption through active and costly reconciliation (and a theology of atonement) – believing that we need not only truth, but also the cross, to be set free. Nonetheless, that contemporary perspective should not obscure the more cautious point, drawn from Illingworth, that knowledge of God and the transformative presence and action of God *may* be discerned in the life of secular society, including in its diversity.

A contemporary critical incarnational theology of chaplaincy

This chapter, therefore, shares some of the aspirations of those earlier Anglican theologians, but seeks also to learn from the critical evaluation of both Ramsey and Temple. The first part of the chapter's theological approach is concerned with a model of dialogue which takes seriously the potential of humanity to reveal something of the nature of Christ. The second part considers shared actions by Christians with those of different faiths as a response to the encounter with Christ in the diversity of humanity, and as engagement with the redemptive purposes of the incarnation.

First, then, in a world starved of theological insight into human nature, including insight into the critical situations in which humanity finds itself at present, this chapter seeks to maximise the opportunity for gathering and sharing insight into the presence and action of God. This recognises that while the God we believe in knows and has revealed in Christ the fullness of divine truth and wisdom, our apprehension of that is boundaried by the limitations of our socio-cultural context. Although we stand in a living tradition rooted in Christ, our membership of that tradition is historically situated. In brief, God's view is universal, but our view (and knowledge of God's view) is partial.

In a plural and pluralistic context, this chapter seeks to offer Christian chaplains (and others engaged in similar theological tasks) a way of envisaging how we may build theological bridges across cultures that respect insight into the divine that comes from different traditions of belief. Fundamental to such an approach is the willingness to engage in dialogue. This involves: first, relationship building, the mutual hospitality characteristic of scriptural reasoning, for example;[2] second, a willingness to listen, as those from different traditions share the wisdom they have discerned; and third, a respectful response.

2   See, for example, www.scripturalreasoning.org.

It may lead to commonly held insight, although that is not expected as an automatic or necessary outcome. What might be expected is that all parties may grow in understanding of their own tradition and its contemporary significance.

Such an approach is to some extent in keeping with Newbigin's understanding of how we live the Christian gospel in a plural society:

> We can and must welcome some measure of plurality because it provides us with a wider range of experience and a wider diversity of human responses to experience, and therefore richer opportunities for testing the sufficiency of our faith than are available in a monochrome society. (Newbigin 2014, pp.243–44)

Where it goes further, however, is in envisaging a mutually enriching process of dialogue, in which those of different faiths and beliefs may grow their understanding of their own tradition. It nonetheless avoids some of Newbigin's concerns about the relativism that he saw as inherent in a pluralistic approach (and rejected) (e.g. 2014, p.244). The model discussed here seeks to move beyond a relativistic understanding that 'truth' is only personal, but at the same time it resists pushing for shared insight at all costs (while allowing that it may result). Neither relativism nor the search for shared truth are allowed to dissolve the differences between the traditions and their particular wisdom. Further, for Christians it anticipates the possibility of a deepening encounter with the incarnate Christ, but does not impose this understanding on the conversation.

This is in keeping with a hopeful but pragmatic approach which holds that, in so far as others will enter into such a search for the truth of human existence, in which participants accompany each other, we can enter into dialogue with them. In this we recognise that they, no less than we, will work from their own tradition, entering into critical dialogue rooted in their own distinct hermeneutic and understanding of wisdom. But the basis for dialogue is the search for greater wisdom and understanding, enriched by journeying together. Clearly this will not work with those who view their apprehension of truth as self-sufficient; nor will it work with those who do not wish to discover deeper wisdom. But chaplains rarely adopt such positions.

Shared conversation, rooted in a commitment to accompany one another on the journey into deeper wisdom and understanding is one strand of the critical incarnational theology of chaplaincy proposed here. But it is only *one* strand. On its own it risks being detached, overly weighted towards cognitive concerns. To make the case for a fully embodied incarnational approach to chaplaincy, dialogue must be brought together with shared action among those involved in chaplaincy teams, again from different faiths and beliefs. In practice, based on both research evidence and wider experience, it seems that chaplaincy is more likely to engage in shared action in multi-faith teams than in sustained dialogue. The position of this chapter is that both are necessary for a fully incarnational approach by Christian chaplains – action also requires dialogue or its description as 'incarnational' lacks theological bite and critical edge.

The argument is that chaplaincies' engagement with those in need is a further aspect, for Christian chaplains, of their encounter with the incarnate Christ. This is in keeping with one reading of Matthew 25.31–46, that interprets 'the least of these my brothers' (v.40; echoed in 'the least of these' in v.45) as meaning everyone, or anyone, in need, not just Christians in need. This follows the interpretation of Davies and Allison (2004, pp.428–29), particularly on the grounds that it is 'all the nations' who are judged, and that it is unlikely (given other references in Matthew to reaching across boundaries) that judgement is only on the basis of the nations' response to Christians, rather than to any in need.

Further, this chapter proposes that this embodied engagement with Christ in the person of those in need extends the more explanatory character of dialogue. The combination of dialogue and pastoral action: a) is properly incarnational, because the wisdom of the incarnation is embodied in action and human presence (in the person of the chaplain and/or those they work with); and b) has obvious potential to be redemptive. The emphasis here on redemption reminds the Christian chaplain (and others) that the incarnation is not just revelatory, in the sense of speaking a word. It is also enacted and embodied redemption, bringing about salvation, healing and reconciliation in the person of Christ, 'the Word made flesh'. This emphasis is partly an answer to Ramsey and Temple, and their concerns noted above – a recognition of a contemporary need for understandings of redemption, that is no less critical now than it was for Temple during the Second World War. Partly it is because redemption is already seen to be a central concern for Christian chaplaincy itself.

As in the case of dialogue, this theology of shared action acknowledges that this is a Christian approach to pastoral care, while those of other traditions will approach from perspectives in keeping with their tradition. The common concern among chaplains of different faiths and beliefs might be articulated as for human wellbeing. This was clearly recognised, for example, by prisoners and prison staff as the primary contribution that chaplaincy makes to the lives of prisoners and the prison (see Todd and Tipton 2011). But for the Christian chaplain, understanding of wellbeing goes hand in hand with a theology of redemption.

Criticality and the need for discernment

But is this broad theological approach also sufficiently robust as a critical tool? Does it also resource the discernment of where God's action or will is frustrated by human action or will – where God's presence does not yet lead to the Kingdom of God being fully realised, or where aspects of the life of society are in need of reconciliation and atonement? Such discernment is, or ought to be, the theological basis for the Christian chaplain's prophetic role; for their speaking out within the host organisation on behalf of the humanity of those whom chaplains serve. To do that effectively the chaplain theologian needs to be an effective interpreter, skilled in the practice of hermeneutics (Todd 2013b, Chapter 9).

The argument of this chapter is that hermeneutics supplies the critical dimension of dialogue and shared action. Such hermeneutics, which interpret the Christian faith today in context, will involve wrestling seriously with different sources of theology. As has already been hinted at, this chapter adopts the Wesleyan Quadrilateral of theological sources: Scripture, tradition, reason and experience (see Outler 1964). This extends the three sources traditionally used in Anglicanism by the addition of 'experience'.[3] As should be clear from the method of this chapter, the balancing of different sources includes giving primacy to Scripture, and paying serious attention to the historic tradition. But it also involves bringing those two into critical correlation with both reason and experience (cf. Browning 1996, pp.44–47; Tracy 1975, pp.43–63) and regarding all four as capable of revealing the presence, action and will of God.

To be critical or prophetic, the conversation from which correlation emerges needs to be robust, especially where the Bible and/or Christian tradition appear to speak with one voice, but experience and reason seem to speak with a different one. A contemporary example (not irrelevant to chaplaincy) of such a critical distance would be between historic Christian understandings of same-sex relations and the contemporary experience and view that they can be a full and good realisation of human personhood and relationship.

To ignore some sources, or even all but one (be it the Bible or contemporary experience), is not rigorous and robust hermeneutics! More particularly, to focus only on historic

---

3   For an Anglican perspective on this addition, see Avis (2014).

sources (Scripture or tradition) is to ignore the continued incarnational presence and action of God in humanity. Uncomfortable though it might be, theological reflection on same-sex relations needs to acknowledge and grapple with the possibility that contemporary scientific understandings of human sexuality are potential sources for that theology. At the same time, the conversation between sources needs to include a critique not only of the historical ones, but also of the contemporary ones – and of the vested interests of all sources.

Chaplains' (or other people's) engagement with all four sources of theology parallels, and elucidates, their embodied engagement in dialogue and action. Drawing on both reason and experience emphasises that neither dialogue, nor action, are sufficient in themselves as ways of being open to God today, but together they represent a thorough engagement with the incarnate Christ (and both have their cognitive and embodied dimensions). This reflects the characteristic engagement of chaplaincy in a plural setting, which begins with being present. Further, the insistence on mutual critique in the correlation of sources, emphasises that dialogue should not slip too easily either into personal opinion, or into common statements that obscure real difference; and it further emphasises that shared action to respond to human need must include openness to those situations where it cannot proceed without serious reconciliatory work.

The implication of the preceding paragraphs is that to engage in robust and critical theology, the Christian chaplain must both inhabit the Christian tradition *and* be thoroughly contextual – and must correlate those two theological approaches as part of one theology. The test of that robustness lies in situations where the dialogue with others includes disagreement, and shared action discerns the need for reconciliation. If that robustness is in place, then the theological approach suggested in this chapter will be sufficiently robust to enable an openness to God in the world that is at the same time critically discerning. And it is from this embodied, critical engagement with all four sources of theology that chaplains and others may work in the midst of complex social settings, where a tension is apparent between contemporary norms and those of the historic Christian tradition.

Pluralism

One remaining question that should be addressed here is the extent to which such a theological approach is amenable to an engagement with pluralism – the valuing of different beliefs. In admitting as source for theology human (rather than just Christian) experience and reason, the above approach opens up a potential engagement with different religious experience, belief and reasoning (e.g. within a multi-faith setting). But it could be seen as still very much an 'inclusivist' approach, in theology of religions terms (see e.g. D'Costa 1986), where the Christian tradition remains the arbiter of truth.

The chaplain might extend beyond such inclusivism in two ways: first, by acknowledging that God's presence, action and will may be known in other religious traditions, but that as a Christian theologian the chaplain's contribution is to interpret what is learnt in a particular situation in the light of their own tradition; second, by being open to the possibility that insight from human reason and experience (including that of those who are not Christian and who interpret human situations in relation to their own faith or belief tradition) may enlarge and therefore change understanding of the Christian tradition. This would seem to be a proper basis for dialogue (and in keeping with, for example, the practice of scriptural reasoning). Both aspects acknowledge the partiality of the chaplain's perspective, discussed above.

Mission

This way of responding to pluralism has further implications for the way in which the theological approach to chaplaincy outlined in this chapter signals a particular missiology. The approach would seem to be in keeping with a missiology rooted in an understanding that mission is primarily an aspect of the way God is and acts – it begins in or with the *missio Dei* (Bosch 1991). In this contemporary model, the Church's responsibility is to discern the mission of God and co-operate with it. Chaplaincy's hermeneutically rooted involvement in dialogue and shared action, and the proposed openness to a pluralistic setting, are in keeping with seeking to discern the *missio Dei*. But they further critique and relocate the wider Church's approach to this model of mission and related understandings of ecclesiology.

The argument is that chaplaincy's discerning the continued incarnational work and presence of God, and the continuing revelation of the transforming purposes of God in diverse social situations and people, is part of a necessary outward movement of mission. This outward movement connects the Church (and its mission) with the present incarnational dimension of the *missio Dei*. Without this connection, gathering as Church is 'excarnational' – out of the body, rather than properly connected with the human body of Christ. This implies an ecclesiology that holds receiving, discerning and dialogue in partnership with celebration (of God's boundless grace); and with proclamation of good news. It is an ecclesiology in which the Church is a sacrament of the Kingdom; an embodied sign of God's presence and action. But in order to be an effective sacrament of Christ's incarnation, the Church must first discern where the incarnation is at work in human social life. To be an effective proclamation of God's good news, the Church must discern where the good news of God is known by the diversity of humanity. Within such an interlinked missiology and ecclesiology, chaplaincy appears central to the Church's identity and purpose, rather than peripheral.

The second effect of this theological understanding of chaplaincy is to critique the way in which different aspects of mission may be construed as a hierarchy, precisely because of an overemphasis on proclamation and gathering. It seems all too easy for church communities and leaders, in a time of numerical decline in congregational numbers, to prioritise those forms of mission that might reverse that decline, or at least ameliorate it. Evangelism, or evangelisation, would be, and is, a prime candidate for such prioritisation. Various attempts have been made to resist such a hierarchy, including the evolution of the five marks of mission, by the Anglican Consultative Council, meeting in 1984. The marks are to:

- proclaim the Good News of the Kingdom

- teach, baptise and nurture new believers

- respond to human need by loving service

- transform unjust structures of society, challenge violence of every kind and pursue peace and reconciliation

- strive to safeguard the integrity of creation, and sustain and renew the life of the earth.[4]

Nonetheless, two aspects of chaplaincy experience suggest that attempts to resist a hierarchy of aspects of mission are only partially successful. One is a continued experience in chaplaincy life and research that church leaders may wish that chaplaincy might contribute rather more directly to numerical and spiritual growth of the Church than they appear to (at least within a short timescale).[5] The second area of experience that Christian chaplains relate is that pastoral care, which for them is primary to their identity, is seen by the wider Church as secondary within mission, or even as

---

4   www.anglicancommunion.org/identity/marks-of-mission.aspx   (accessed   10 October 2016).
5   See further Todd, Slater and Dunlop 2014, pp.29–35.

not being to do with mission at all. The argument of this chapter is that this view needs to be subject to the critique of chaplaincy and a commitment to discerning the *missio Dei* that is in keeping with a theology of God's presence and action in the world.

In the interest of this rebalancing of understandings of mission, it is worth revisiting the outcome of mission. The argument might run that the primary outcome of mission is the primary outcome of the *missio Dei*; that understanding that primary outcome in too ecclesiological a way (as conversion, for example) is too proximate, and rather that a more genuinely theological way of construing the outcome is required, such as redemption – that which God brings about in continued interaction with creation.

It would follow from this that if pastoral care is redemptive (resulting in healing, reconciliation or other human transformation), then it may be discerned as a primary form of mission, a true participation by those involved in God's mission. This is not to say that evangelism/evangelisation are not also primary aspects of mission, nor to say that conversion may not be an aspect of human redemption. But it is to question the criteria by which we discern what is mission, and to critique any exclusive emphasis in mission on proclamation, at the expense of including pastoral care as a full player in the economy of mission.

There is a similar argument for fully incorporating dialogue in the economy of mission. Indeed, dialogue is itself a 'mixed economy' within the wider picture. On the one hand, it can be discerned to be in keeping with, and more particularly a discovery of, God present and at work. On the other hand, dialogue necessarily involves some telling of the Christian tradition – this is part of engaging hermeneutically in dialogue. So, dialogue can connect insight gained from those of diverse cultures, beliefs and practices with the wisdom of the gospel.

This argument in turn supports a reworking, at the ecclesiological level, of the economy of ministry. If engagement in mission is a criterion for effective ministry, then chaplaincy, on the basis of its record of pastoral care alone, is effective ministry. The implications of this for an understanding of the diversity of the ministry of the whole people of God are significant, placing those who listen and engage in dialogue alongside those who proclaim; those who care alongside those who interpret; and those who discover God in diverse social settings alongside those who gather people to celebrate the same God in the worshipping life of the Church.

Conclusion

This chapter has offered a thoroughly reworked incarnational theology of chaplaincy. The primary direction of this theology is towards the discernment of the incarnate Christ within the diversity of humanity (while recognising that this sits in a wider Trinitarian frame). The chapter proposes two particular ways in which this theology is realised: through dialogue and pastoral care (seen especially as shared action). Together these offer two important dimensions of a fully embodied engagement with God in a plural and pluralistic world. They enable a fully critical hermeneutic, involving four sources of theology: Scripture, tradition, reason and experience. The two dimensions do not represent the totality of chaplaincy practice, nor do they preclude chaplains engaging in other aspects of mission. But they do represent chaplaincy at its most incarnational.

The chapter continued by drawing parallels with an approach to mission, that begins with discerning the *missio Dei*, the redemptive work of God in diverse social settings and people's lives. That pastoral care and dialogue may be seen as key aspects of this discernment and realisation of redemption suggested a rebalancing of the Church's economy of mission, in which the outward movement, characterised by open eyes and listening ears, should be understood as working in harmony with movements of proclamation and gathering. The chapter offers, therefore, a theology of the world, with the aim of enabling chaplains and others to discern the presence, action and will of God in diverse social settings and how to work with God in those places.

References

Avis, P. (2014) *In Search of Authority: Anglican Theological Method from the Reformation to the Enlightenment*. London: Bloomsbury/T&T Clark.

Beckford, J.A. (2003) *Social Theory and Religion*. Cambridge: Cambridge University Press.

Bosch, D. (1991) *Transforming Mission: Paradigm Shifts in Theology of Mission*. New edition. Maryknoll, NY: Orbis Books.

Browning, D.S. (1996) *A Fundamental Practical Theology: Descriptive and Strategic Proposals*. Minneapolis: Fortress Press.

Davies, W.D. and Allison, D.C. (2004) *A Critical and Exegetical Commentary on the Gospel According to Saint Matthew. The International Critical Commentary on the Holy Scriptures of the Old and New Testaments*. London, New York: T&T Clark International.

D'Costa, G. (1986) *Theology and Religious Pluralism*. Oxford: Blackwell.

Gilliat-Ray, S., Ali, M.M. and Pattison, S. (2013) *Understanding Muslim Chaplaincy*. Aldershot: Ashgate.

Gore, C. (ed.) (1904) *Lux Mundi: A Series of Studies in the Religion of the Incarnation*. 15th edition. London: John Murray.

Illingworth, J.R. (1904) 'The Incarnation in Relation to Development.' In C. Gore (ed.) *Lux Mundi: A Series of Studies in the Religion of the Incarnation*. 15th edition. London: John Murray.

Newbigin, L. (2014) *The Gospel in a Pluralist Society*. New York: SPCK Classics.

Outler, Albert C. (ed.) (1964) *John Wesley*. New York: Oxford University Press.

Ramsey, M. (1960) *From Gore to Temple: The Development of Anglican Theology Between Lux Mundi and the Second World War, 1889–1939*. London: Longmans.

Ryan, B. (2015) *A Very Modern Ministry: Chaplaincy in the UK*. London: Theos.

Todd, A. (2011) 'Responding to Diversity: Chaplaincy in a Multi-Faith Context.' In M. Threlfall-Holmes and M. Newitt (2011) *Being a Chaplain*. London: SPCK.

Todd, A. (2013a) 'Preventing the "neutral" chaplain?: the potential impact of anti-"extremism" policy on prison chaplaincy.' *Practical Theology* 6 (2): 144–58.

Todd, A. (ed.) (2013b) *Military Chaplaincy in Contention: Chaplains, Churches, and the Morality of Conflict. Explorations in Practical, Pastoral, and Empirical Theology*. Burlington, VT: Ashgate.

Todd, A. (2014) 'Religion, security, rights, the individual and rates of exchange: religion in negotiation with British public policy in prisons and the military.' *International Journal of Politics, Culture, and Society* 28 (1): 37–50.

Todd, A. and Tipton, L. (2011) *The Role and Contribution of a Multi-Faith Prison Chaplaincy to the Contemporary Prison Service*. Available at: www.stpadarns. ac.uk/wp-content/uploads/2016/06/Todd-and-Tipton-2011-Report-on-Prison-Chaplaincy-1.pdf.

Todd, A., Slater, V. and Dunlop, S. (2014) *The Church of England's Involvement in Chaplaincy: Research Report for the Church of England's Mission and Public Affairs Council.* Accessed on 7/7/2017 at: http://orca.cf.ac.uk/62257.

Torry, M. (2010) *Bridgebuilders: Workplace Chaplaincy – A History.* Norwich: Canterbury Press Norwich.

Tracy, D. (1975) *Blessed Rage for Order.* Minneapolis: Seabury Press.

2

TWENTY-FIRST CENTURY CHAPLAINCY

Finding the Church in the Post-Secular

——————— JAMES WALTERS ———————

Chaplaincy as the locus of Church/world relations

This book reflects a growing interest in chaplaincy at the present time and a recognition of the need to offer some theological underpinning for the diverse forms of ministry it is generating. Chaplaincy arrangements are usually pragmatic and contextual. They evolve in response to circumstances and institutional particularities. But a wide range of people, from church leaders to policy researchers, are now asking questions about the overarching character and objectives of chaplaincy. It has become the object of many studies and reports with a wide range of different objectives identified in different sectors. With National Health Service (NHS) resources under increasing pressure, there has been assessment of the role that healthcare chaplaincy might make to clinical outcomes. In my own sector of higher education where chaplaincy is not statutory, government guidelines have recently pointed to the role chaplaincy might play in countering religious radicalisation. And across the public sector, institutions are considering how chaplains might enable them to meet the requirements of equality legislation to eliminate discrimination on the grounds of religion and belief.

However, this chapter puts these institutional agendas to one side and takes up the theological considerations of the Church's interest in, and understanding of, chaplaincy. It will seek to locate the work of chaplains in the public sphere within the mission and identity of the whole Church of God. This theological task is timely since the renewed interest in chaplaincy may reflect a final overcoming of the sense of chaplaincy as the poor relation to the Church's parochial ministry. But there are also dangers that the new championing of chaplaincy has a cruder pragmatic rationale. If chaplaincy is now more central in the Church's agenda, it has to be said that this arises largely from the fact that, while overall church attendance continues to decline, chaplaincy is growing. A recent report by the religion thinktank Theos found a dramatic growth in chaplaincy provision in the UK, with diverse forms of chaplaincy 'expanding into ever more fields' (Ryan 2015, p.8). We will come on to consider the reasons for this growth.

I want to begin by suggesting, however, that chaplaincy is of particular theological interest because it concentrates the question that modernity has rendered so problematic, which is the relation of the Church to the world. Western Europeans defined their modernity by removing the Church from the public square (or thinking they had). The ever-greater privatisation of faith through the modern era led to the consensus 'that religions were about what people did with their solitude' (Wright 2016, p.14). To most people in Britain today, the Church is an institution of marginal significance and the legacies of its more prominent role (Bishops in the House of Lords, the preponderance of church schools) appear antiquated and anachronistic. Equally it would seem that many Christians themselves are similarly defining the Church by keeping the world at arm's length. Many have retreated into a narrow gospel of 'pie in the sky when you die' with little account of how the Kingdom that Jesus proclaimed might be realised in this world. A complex, multi-faith society with a rise in permissive social values is not one in which many Christians find it easy to make connections between their faith and the wider public sphere. The relationship of Church and world is the most fraught issue for Christian theology today and has been for some time. It was articulated lucidly by the father of Liberation Theology, Gustavo Gutiérrez in 1988:

> We are faced on the one hand with the affirmation of an ever more autonomous world, not religious, or in more positive terms, a world come of age. On the other hand we are also faced with this single vocation to salvation which values human history in Christian terms, although in a way different from that of the past. Caught in this pincerlike movement, which was not exempt from misinterpretation and sloppy expression, the distinction of planes appears as a burnt out model with nothing to say to the advances in theological thinking. (Gutiérrez 1988, p.46)

Part of the reason why chaplaincy is so interesting is that it represents myriad case studies of reintegrating these planes. Each chaplaincy attempts to broker a renewed relationship between Church and world. This is why it is impossible to talk about a single theology of chaplaincy or a single model of chaplaincy. Every chaplain is an attempt to integrate sacred and secular, eternal and temporal, Church and world. And we all do it in different ways, reflecting the complexity of late modern British society and its relationship to the Church. There are chaplaincies that represent a very traditional and idealist understanding of the Christian society. Think of a public-school chaplain who presides over Matins from the Book of Common Prayer every morning. That reflects the national religion model of integrating Church and world, common to several European countries but particularly characterised by the Church of England and its state-authorised liturgy. Contrast that chaplain with an NHS chaplain who is part of a multi-faith team and whose focus is on the spiritual wellbeing of the sick and dying. Reflecting a more pluralist modern Britain, it may be unclear whether there is or ought to be a Christian priority within that chaplaincy team. And if there is, is that simply numerically based? Will the priority end if Christians become less than 50 per cent of the population? This chaplain may or may not be linked to a parish church. The chaplain may or may not have regular services within the hospital. Then there are the altogether more postmodern forms of chaplaincy to organisations or facilities not formerly the focus of the Church's concern, such as railway stations or shopping centres. There are chaplains who may have little association with traditional religious institutions, even described as 'generic'. Each of these are different responses to the crisis of Church/world relations, configuring it in a different way and forming an appropriate bridge.

Church/world relations in the post-secular

A particularly interesting development of our time is that the disconnection of Church and world that modernity appeared to necessitate is now being challenged by some resurgence of religion in the public sphere. German philosopher Jürgen Habermas has even suggested that we are in a post-secular age (Habermas 2008). This is a contentious claim, but the dramatic growth in chaplaincy appears to support this view. We need to define the post-secular in two ways.

First, and most obviously, the assumption of Western European elites, informed by Weberian sociology, that secularisation went hand in hand with economic and social development has been disproved. On the contrary, globally secularisation has gone into reverse. Data published in 2015 by the Pew Research Center suggests that by 2050 the proportion of the world's population that has no religious affiliation will drop from 16 to 13 per cent (Pew Research Center 2015). This is due, first, to demographics. Less religious parts of the world such as Europe are not reproducing as fast as the religious ones such as Africa and Latin America. Second, it is due to particular forms of religious fervour and radicalisation across all the world religions. Islam is the most publicised example but Pentecostalism, Hindu Nationalism and even religious Zionism are all making religion more central to people's self-understanding at a time when other sources of identity, such as nation and race, may be of diminished significance. And third, desecularisation is due to the spread of democracy and the fall of Communism. Christianity has grown fastest in recent decades in parts of the world where religion had long been outlawed, most notably China.

So while many of us in the Church of England are still trapped in the mentality of universal decline, the global picture is very different. Christianity has a very promising future, particularly in Sub-Saharan Africa and Latin America. But we are experiencing the effects of that too, particularly at the points of global intersection. That is true of the Diocese of London where church attendance has been increasing by 2.5 per cent each year. But it is also true in many public institutions, such as universities, which chaplains serve. The London School of Economics draws two-thirds of its students from overseas, from a total of over 150 different countries. It has been a source of much bafflement to many of our academics that the student body is significantly more religious than the faculty. So I, like many chaplains, am working in a context in which religion is unexpectedly resurgent and requires both provision of various kinds and some kind of co-ordination to foster a culture where that religious pluralism can hold together.

Second, the post-secular should be defined in terms of some kind of crisis of secular coherence. Chaplaincy is an expression of the Church's relationship with institutions that the Church does not govern. Some of them – like a university, perhaps a hospital – have even sought to define themselves to some degree against the superstitious thinking with which religion is associated. But across the board today we are seeing a crisis of meaning within those institutions, with fundamental questions being asked about their purpose. Do universities simply exist to increase a young person's earning potential and make them more competitive in a growing market economy? Does a hospital exist simply to keep people alive as long as possible, with little consideration given to care, quality of life, or even preparation for the inevitability of death? Do prisons exist simply to contain dangerous people as an enterprise that can generate profit for the private sector? All of these questions are being asked as symptoms of the crisis of modern secular institutions. So chaplaincy is of interest because it is also raising the question of the Church's contribution to the renewal of public institutions in the post-secular era.

Where does the chaplain stand?

To understand how this, and the Church's other missionary endeavours, might be pursued through chaplaincy, we need to look more closely at the models of Church/world relations that the person of the chaplain can represent. To do that I want to ask the questions: where does the chaplain stand and what might this tell us about the ecclesiology of the chaplain's ministry?

Turning your back to the Church

Some might say that the chaplain stands with her back to the Church. They might say that either critically or approvingly. Negatively, there has been a perception that chaplaincy is some kind of 'escape from the church', from the demands of parish ministry and the immediate oversight of the bishop and the diocese. Chaplaincy may appear to offer a better work–life balance and greater freedom. I think there are some questions about the sustainability of the demands made on parish clergy and there is certainly an under-explored issue of the protections afforded by equality legislation to sections of the clergy working in secular institutions that are not available to parish clergy. But let us be clear that chaplaincy has its own challenges, expects high professional standards and can be far more demanding in terms of energy and intensity than many parishes.

But these days, a chaplain might also be deemed to have turned his back on the Church positively for evangelistic reasons. Chaplaincy now sometimes falls in the category of 'fresh expressions' or 'pioneer ministry' that is deemed to benefit from being unencumbered by the Church's structures and tradition. The Theos report into chaplaincy identified a particular ministry 'that goes to where people actually are, rather than waiting for them to come to religion' (Ryan 2015, p.79). Anxiety about proselytism can bring tensions here. Most chaplains recognise that credibility within their institution is dependent on their not being seen to have conversion of non-Christians as a primary goal. But opportunities for responding to spiritual curiosity with new forms of Church do present themselves, such as in the collaboration of London university chaplains to begin The Anchorage, a new worshipping community for students built around community, exploration of the Christian faith, informal worship and social action (www.theanchoragelondon.org).

The success of such experiments will depend in the long term, however, not on their separation from the mainstream church but on the strength of the contribution they make to the whole as they are incorporated into the common ecclesial life. The fissure between Church and world will not be overcome by going totally native. Chaplains who have their back to the Church are cut off from the source of their identity, the community of wisdom and sacramental transformation, to the detriment of their own spiritual lives and that of the people they serve.

In the world facing the Church

A better model might be, therefore, to say that the chaplain stands in the world facing the Church. This could be seen as the chaplain as missioner, sent out as sheep among wolves to point to the sacred from within the secular. The emphasis might be on witness, Christian nurture, teaching and sacramental provision. This is the model adopted by Roman Catholic colleagues with whom I have served. Their ministry has been to serve and grow the Catholic community within the university, pointing them towards the Church and forming them in its teaching. It is a perfectly coherent model that recognises the Church as 'home', the community of redemption into which converts are drawn. But it is, therefore, liable to a sectarian suspicion of the world and can be ill-equipped to respond to the post-secular changes I outlined earlier. It very much confines chaplaincy to an arena that is of little relevance to the rest of the institution and may sometimes even harbour suspicion of other faith communities.

Looking both ways

So is the chaplain standing between Church and world, looking both ways? Sometimes chaplains are described as bilingual people having to translate the language of one institution to the other, and I certainly recognise something of that. One of the most important contributions of chaplaincy is to bring the voices of the world into conversation with the Church and articulate Christian wisdom within that context too. Serving a social science university, I am particularly mindful of the role that the empirical study of social inequality played in fashioning Liberation Theology's response to the problem Gutiérrez sets out above. Chaplaincy should break down some of the accumulated suspicion that sacred and secular discourses have for one another, doing so with the renewed confidence that post-secularity has overcome, 'as a primary challenge, the unquestioned hegemony of secular modes of practice and discourse' (Muers in Greggs, Muers and Zahl 2003, p.246).

Nonetheless, for me, this model of facing both ways implies too much of an opposition between Church and world. We should not forget that the Church is already present in the secular institutions we serve in the form of Christian laypeople who work in them or use them. Clerical colleagues who pity my having to minister in an institution with associations of atheism and political radicalism are astonished to learn that a recent LSE director began his address to the student interfaith forum with the words, 'As a practising Christian, I want to encourage the work of this forum...' The post-secular is reminding us that the secular was never quite as secular as we thought and many believers have quietly contributed their faith and values to sustaining public institutions in ways we have failed to acknowledge. Neither is the world absent from the worshipping church, as we shall consider in a moment. This strong opposition is unhelpful and chaplains should not feel schizophrenic.

Standing in the world as the Church, looking around

The model I favour is that the chaplain stands in the world, as a representative of the Church, *looking around*. In contrast to the views of some, I have found that the representational dimensions of the priesthood in chaplaincy are more intensified than in the parish. You represent the Church among many people who have no other encounter with it. And so you are called to immerse yourself fully in the life of a secular institution while witnessing the transformative love of Christ that the Church represents. You are not there to condemn the world but to love it and serve it (John 3.16). And I believe that the Church provides chaplains, not to any institution, but to those within which we can identify the transformative work of the Spirit bringing about the Kingdom of God. The chaplain looks around and sees where that work is taking place, draws it out and seeks to make it fruitful.

The theology of chaplaincy is incarnational, as my description of chaplaincy as the reconciliation of temporal and eternal implied. But it seems rather curious to me that when people use the language of incarnation they often seem to imply something quite static and passive. The incarnation was temporally involved and dynamic: healing, serving, teaching, transforming. We need to move beyond the maxim that I have heard more than one chaplain quote, that we are simply in the business of 'keeping the rumour of God alive'. That was never adequate and the post-secular paradigm offers us far more potential for transformative action as representatives of the Church in the world looking around and cultivating the seeds of the Kingdom.

The marks of the Church in chaplaincy

Implicit in my argument is that modernity polarised the Church/world question in a rather unhelpful way. Pre-modernity was not like that. As John Milbank famously wrote, 'Once there was no secular.'[1] Now we are again moving into an era where the secular world need not simply be viewed as a barren, threatening mission field. We are certainly not reverting to Christendom. But the climate has changed and the Church's engagement with these kinds of post-secular environments needs to begin with a less oppositional view of the world, one more open to the signs of God around us. Writing as the Nazis came to power in Germany, Lutheran theologian Dietrich Bonhoeffer had much cause to demonise the world. Yet he describes the Church simply as 'the place

---

1   This is the opening line of John Milbank's radical reappraisal of modern thought, *Theology and Social Theory: Beyond Secular Reason* (Oxford: Wiley-Blackwell 2006, 2nd edition).

– that is, the space – in the world where the reign of Jesus Christ over the whole world is to be demonstrated and proclaimed' (Bonhoeffer 2005, p.63). The world is imbued with divine potentiality and we identify the Church as the locations where that is drawn out and made present in signs of grace and transformation. These are the opportunities for action that the chaplain is looking for within the secular institution she serves and they are precisely those moments where the Church – as agent of the Kingdom – becomes possible.

To give this definition more substance, those moments will exhibit the qualities of the four marks of the Church. I want to conclude, therefore, by drawing together some thoughts on how those marks are exhibited in the kind of Church/world relation that I have expressed.

One

The chaplain is called to exhibit the unitive ministry of Christ. This is the Christ who drew all people to himself on the cross (John 12.32), the Christ who has gathered all things together in himself (Ephesians 1.10). The chaplain can be a sort of institutional glue, bringing different sections of the community together, or at very least connecting them through her own relationships with people at different levels of the organisation. The chaplain who is available to all from the Vice Chancellor to the porter gives people a sense of belonging and interconnectedness. In his encounters with diverse people in the Gospels, Jesus connects people to one another through his mediatory role with the Father. All are one because all are created and redeemed by the one God. Even when it is inappropriate to articulate this verbally, the iconography of chaplaincy is constantly signifying this: the worth of all people and the interrelation of all people.

The activities of chaplains are instruments of unity. I recall the governor of a prison attending a service on

Christmas morning alongside the prisoners, celebrated by the prison chaplain. I have seen the way hospital chaplains can be the ones who draw together patient, family and medical staff at moments of trauma. For many chaplains in contemporary, multi-faith public institutions, the challenge of unity is an increasingly interfaith task. This is dealt with more explicitly in other chapters of this book. But we should simply note here that while it is clearly not the case that the Church could be constituted by adherents of different creeds, the unitive mission of the Church spills over into the task of reconciliation in the world, including the reconciliation between religions that is so desperately needed in our age. University chaplains promoting interfaith dialogue are often met with suspicion by conservative Christians who quote John 14.6, 'I am the way and the truth and the life. No one comes to the Father except through me.' But Rupert Shortt suggests these students need to be referred back to their Bibles:

> The 'me' referred to here is none other than the Word of God who enlightens the hearts of all people, as the prologue to the fourth Gospel makes clear... [Christian faith] entails a confidence that all human beings possess a basic dignity, regardless of local differences, which renders the goal of universal reconciliation and universal fellowship conceivable in the first place. (Shortt 2016, p.62)

The chaplain is one who brings universal reconciliation and universal fellowship as an expression of the unity of the Church.

Holy

It cannot be overstated that the chaplain's unitive activities are not simply achieved through strength of personality or pastoral manner. It is a consequence of the chaplain's representational role. The chaplain represents the God in whom each individual finds their sense of self and purpose, even for many who will not think of it at all in those terms. The loss of the transcendent is precisely where secular institutions have gone awry, because, in transcendence, we are not talking about an imaginary man in the sky whose loss is of no consequence. We are talking about the transcendent origin of the values that give coherence to both institutional and individual lives.

Take, for example, the university itself. Founded by monastic communities in Bologna and Paris in the twelfth century, these centres of learning were expressions of a theological belief in the universality of knowledge that was inextricably linked to the belief in one God and one baptism for all believers. The university, at its origin, espoused a profoundly theological understanding of reason, set out so comprehensively in Cardinal Newman's *The Idea of a University* (Newman 1996). We should not be surprised, therefore, that in today's radically instrumentalised higher education culture, many are lamenting a constriction of thinking and the compartmentalisation of disciplines. The loss of transcendence, or holiness, has diminished our self-understanding, both personally and institutionally.

In our post-secular context, an awareness is being expressed of the failure of purely utilitarian thinking. But few advocate a return to theological foundations and a transcendence that ensured meaning. It is imperative, therefore, that the chaplain represents and transmits holiness in his presence, his actions and his leading of worship and prayer. This is a profound witness to what has been lost, and may yet be recovered, in the post-secular context.

Catholic

To be an agent of catholicity in this context has a lot to do with the holding together of pluralism. The Church is constituted by the holding together of difference and the representative of the Church in the secular institution needs to give energy and vision to articulating how cohesive pluralism can work. The world is now constantly talking about 'equality and diversity' but it cannot see beyond how such goods are fostered apart from a combative discourse of human rights. Recent New Testament scholarship has emphasised how the gathering of very different people within the highly stratified society of the Roman Empire was the unique gift of Christianity to the Ancient World. The word *ekklesia*, used by the Early Christians to designate their gatherings, means 'citizens' assembly' and expresses the radical inclusion that Christianity made possible in a world where citizenship was a privilege for the few and many did not even own their own lives. The catholicity of the Church was a disturbing new idea (see especially Williams 2015).

Catholicity may be the Church's greatest gift to public institutions in our age. A recognition of the contribution of different groups as a celebration of diversity needs to evolve into a more New Testament vision of interdependence and mutual flourishing. Chaplains should advocate for minority groups but also seek to overcome the competitive narratives of victimhood that further fragment. Identity politics has become unhelpfully shrill, particularly on university campuses. We are increasingly aware of discrimination suffered by black people, the transgendered, minority religious groups and so on. But this is also feeding a culture of blame, accusation and suspicion. Chaplains can help build common cause by championing the inclusion of all in ways that do not set groups against one another, recognising the distinctively Pauline insight that the suffering of the weakest member damages the whole body (1 Corinthians 12.21–27).

Apostolic

Finally, we might consider that an important aspect of the apostolic ministry of the chaplain in this post-secular age is to find opportunities to contribute to the re-articulation of institutional vocation. As I said earlier, the justification for chaplains ought not simply to be evangelistic opportunity. We need missioners and evangelists for that. We have chaplains to institutions that we believe further the Kingdom of God in disseminating wisdom and learning, in healing the sick, in reforming the sinner and so on. The chaplain has the task, therefore, of raising up that institution to find its calling (Ephesians 4.13) such that, while there is no question of the Church colonising or governing it, it recovers some sense of being a secular agent of grace. Thus in the exercise of the chaplain's own apostolic ministry she also contributes to the renewal of her institution's mission and calling beyond instrumentalism and market logic. In some contexts, such as in a university, that may be organising events or lectures to explore the vocation of the institution from a theological perspective to see what wisdom that might bring. In others, it may be informal conversations of provocative encouragement with those charged with running public institutions in times of high bureaucratic demands and thinly spread resource. To be an apostle is to be someone sent with a purpose. In an age of profound confusion about the common good, we can help the institutions we serve to ask what it is they have been 'sent' to do.

In attributing the marks of the Church to the chaplain's work in this way, I do not want to imply the total collapse of the Church/world polarity and I certainly do not mean to secularise the character of the Church. The historic British churches are in a time when numerical growth in church attendance is important. Chaplains need to lead those who are seeking faith in Christ to baptism and encourage nominal believers to engage with the life of the Church outside the institution. But we do need to be less stark in our Church/world opposition and see the secular as an arena in which the fruits of the Church can be brought forth for the sake of the Kingdom that is the flourishing of the institutions we serve. As a representative of the Church, immersed in the life of the world and looking for the signs of the activity of God, the chaplain has a crucial role to play in the renewal both of the Church and of public life in this post-secular era.

References

Bonhoeffer, D. (2005) *Ethics.* Minneapolis, MN: Fortress Press.

Greggs, T., Muers, R. and Zahl, S. (2003) *The Vocation of Theology Today.* London: Cascade Books.

Gutiérrez, G. (1988) *A Theology of Liberation.* New York: Orbis Books.

Habermas, J. (2008) *Between Naturalism and Religion: Philosophical Essays.* London: Polity Press.

Newman, J.H. (1996) *The Idea of a University.* New Haven, CT: Yale University Press.

Pew Research Center (2015) *The Future of World Religions: Population Growth Projections 2010–2050.* Accessed on 7/7/2017 at: www.pewforum.org/2015/04/02/religious-projections-2010-2050.

Ryan, B. (2015) *A Very Modern Ministry: Chaplaincy in the UK.* London: Theos.

Shortt, R. (2016) *God is No Thing: Coherent Christianity.* London: Hurst and Co.

Williams, R. (2015) *Meeting God in Paul.* London: SPCK.

Wright, T. (2016) *God in Public: How the Bible Speaks Truth to Power Today.* London: SPCK.

3

'ALL FAITHS AND NONE?'

Theological Issues in Multi-Faith Chaplaincy

———————— ROWAN WILLIAMS ————————

In his 2008 report *Faiths in Higher Education Chaplaincy*, Jeremy Clines includes a section on 'the chaplain as theologian' (Clines 2008, p.38ff). He acknowledges a particular need for a coherent theology that informs and resources the praxis of Christian chaplains working in multi-faith contexts: if chaplaincy is the public face of faith in a diverse and plural society, it needs to engage with those of all faiths and none. Clines does not articulate such a theology himself, but recognises that for the Christian chaplain, the theological resources of our own tradition can provide a helpful framework within which to exercise such a ministry with integrity.

Two recent publications on chaplaincy (Ryan 2015; Slater 2015) both question whether chaplaincy needs to be rooted in an institution or organisation; evolving models of community-based chaplaincy express a pastoral relationship which may or may not have an explicit faith component. My own experience is of providing chaplaincy to *institutions*, working both in ecumenical and multi-faith teams in educational and healthcare settings. It is out of that experience that my theological reflection on chaplaincy is formed. I write also as a Catholic Anglican, for whom it is essential that the particular ministry of chaplaincy is exercised and rooted in relationship with the institutional Church, as well as within the parameters of doctrinally orthodox Christian faith. Legood (1999), while now rather out of date in many of his assumptions about how chaplains relate to their context, takes the ecclesiological implications of chaplaincy particularly seriously.

It is important to begin by distinguishing ecumenical from multi-faith chaplaincy. Conversations on the nature and identity of God between members of different Christian denominations must clearly begin in a different place from those which are possible between Christians and members of other faiths. Multi-faith dialogue worthy of the name has to begin with an honest acknowledgement of very real differences: between respective views of God, of Christ, of Scripture, and of worship. It may still choose to celebrate those things we have in common, but any genuine dialogue must also confront the reality of difference, without necessarily finding it threatening or excluding.

Though the word 'chaplaincy' itself derives from the legend of St Martin of Tours sharing his cloak (*capella*) with a person in need, the twenty-first century context of chaplaincy to secular institutions is no longer one in which Christian models or understandings can be taken for granted. Within other faith communities, the Christian etymology of 'chaplaincy' can be problematic, in that it immediately evokes a Christian-centric understanding of the world (cf. *A Very Modern Ministry*, p.11), but there is as yet no universally agreed alternative. A distinctive Muslim chaplaincy is still developing, but the training provided by the Markfield Institute and the Association of Muslim Chaplains has gone some way towards assuring institutions that Muslim chaplains will work within the 'all faiths and none' framework for its own sake, rather than merely adopting a praxis shaped by Christian assumptions, or ministering only to members of their own faith community (Gilliat-Ray, Ali and Pattison 2013, p.8).

Nevertheless, Christian chaplains still need to find a way to articulate their role with a sense of personal and theological integrity drawn from their own tradition. The aim of this chapter is not to create one overarching theology of multi-faith chaplaincy, even supposing that were possible, but rather to begin to articulate a Christian theology of multi-faith engagement, which in turn might provide a plausible practical framework for Christian chaplains whose role is to represent the Christian faith, and the Christian community, alongside colleagues of other faiths within a particular context. With this end in mind, I shall provide an overview, from a Trinitarian Christian perspective, of some pressing *theological* issues which face Christian chaplains working in multi-faith teams. I shall then examine two major issues of both theological and practical significance for all who work in a multi-faith context: team leadership and the negotiated use of shared space.

Truth, catholicity and universality

The central theological issue for any multi-faith engagement must concern the nature of truth, as revealed by our respective understandings of the nature of God. The difficulty of doing theology in multi-faith chaplaincy thus begins with language: what do we *mean* by God? If we have no common language about or concept of God, it is difficult to imagine how it might be possible to do 'theo-logy' (literally, to speak about God) together with others. At the same time, if the existence of God is considered to be *the* absolute truth which nearly all faiths share, it is important to find ways to explore how differing faith perspectives help to illuminate or obscure that truth for each other. Writing in the context of higher education chaplaincy, Clines (2008) stresses the value of pursuing truth in community with others, following Newman (1852 [1996]) in arguing that the pursuit of truth is the central ideal around which universities were formed, and which continues to shape their purpose in a plural world.

All the major world faiths can relate to some degree to the assertion that God is One: big enough simultaneously to encompass all the varied conceptions of divinity, and not to be confined or restricted by them. This approach is obviously more problematic for some groups who might prefer the description 'worldview' or 'standpoint' to that of 'faith' or 'religion', or whose very breadth of identity does not allow for easy categorisation. Some forms of Buddhism, for example, would not necessarily embrace theism, nor even deism, and would therefore not describe Buddhism as a faith, while others are more comfortable with such language. So claiming that an awareness of 'God' can create common ground or the locus of unity in diversity may be inappropriate for them, as it also would be for any humanist or atheist chaplain. The same breadth can also be found within Quakerism, for example: some Quakers are quite happy to identify themselves as Christians, albeit of a deliberately non-dogmatic and non-doctrinal kind, while others would struggle with that designation: the title 'chaplain' can sometimes be problematic for them because of its links with institutional Christianity.[1] However, if even the atheist polemicist Sam Harris can write about transcendent experience without wishing to ascribe it to any kind of divinity (Harris 2014), there is clearly space for those who *do* claim a religious identity, however disparate, to explore together the unifying potential of otherness or beyondness.

It may not be possible to personify or define such a sense of otherness in a way which is genuinely universal. Nevertheless, I would want to argue that the very transcendent otherness and beyondness which is part of the identity of the Christian God also means that it is possible to unite members of different faiths around the proposition that God is 'essentially unknowable'.[2] Although that is not the whole truth for

---

1 The Quaker website, www.quaker.org.uk/about-quakers (accessed 10 October 2016), describes Quakerism as a faith, but makes it clear that the emphasis is on personal experience and righteous action 'rooted in the divine', rather than adherence to an externally defined orthodoxy.

2 Lipner (1994) explores at some length the complexity of the Hindu conception of deity and divinity. 'Dogmatic affirmations concerning the nature of God' are to be avoided (p.2), but his identification of the devas as 'personified focuses of the transcendent' allows for a monotheistic understanding of an essentially unknowable God (p.29).

Christians, the unknowability and indefinability of the divine nevertheless provides a potential lens through which we can dare to explore our differing perspectives on truth. Each religious or spiritual tradition, including those that would struggle with the concept of Godhead revealed through incarnation, makes space (albeit sometimes a contested or 'suspect' space) for encounter with the unknowable through mysticism, apophasis and transcendent otherness. Multi-faith chaplaincy teams may have to decide whether even to attempt to enter this space together in worship and if they do choose to do so, will need to agree on how to enable differing traditions to participate with integrity.

Words, images and rituals all have obvious limitations as vehicles for shared worship; they are not neutral, but freighted with a range of significance and interpretation. While the same is true of silence, it is at least possible that praying or meditating in silence together might potentially open up a shared experience of creating space which it is possible for each participant to acknowledge as sacred, without seeking to define too narrowly or exclusively what that might mean. Through that shared experience of sacred space, it might then be possible to enter into encounter with the divine in the presence of others who are doing the same thing; the fact that they are doing so from within a different set of understandings of what is happening can then be acknowledged and honoured, without actually becoming a barrier. While some Christians find this unacceptable, in that it gives at least tacit legitimacy to beliefs they do not hold to be true, others welcome it as the locus of a shared experience of the divine which defies categorisation. Another potential avenue for exploration in this area is the growing popularity of mindfulness and meditation in secular environments. Although this too is open to question in some quarters, the fact that it is not owned by, or aligned with, any one religious or spiritual tradition might allow the Christian chaplain to offer what is effectively silent contemplation without either compromising their own beliefs, or offending the sensibilities of others.

The apophatic tradition, to an extent, relies on an awareness of *absence*, or at least of implied absence. Of course, that does not mean that God really is absent; but the true value and the true content of apophatic silence is that each participant, from within their own tradition, becomes conscious of the limitations of their own ability to perceive, still less to describe, what God is like. Whether it is labelled mindfulness, meditation, contemplation or apophasis is less important than the opportunity it affords each person to come into contact with their own powerlessness, their own inability and their own need of something or someone beyond themselves – and to realise that this experience of insufficiency is universal.

However, as soon as silence is replaced by words, the challenge posed by the different faiths' varied understandings of God cannot merely be brushed aside. Genuine multi-faith working requires a willingness to risk entering into dialogue, discussion and a mode of team-working which engages with the biggest questions. The practice of scriptural reasoning, in which members of different faith groups present their sacred texts to each other on their own terms, is a particularly potent way to approach this. Differing approaches to scriptural authority and religious truth, both within and between traditions, affect praxis in chaplaincy. The importance of learning to disagree well, while simultaneously respecting the integrity of others and not compromising one's own identity, has been an increasingly prominent feature of recent Anglican ecclesiology, which might prove equally fruitful in interfaith (and interdenominational!) dialogue (See Faith and Order Commission 2016).

Being honest about the fact that members of different faiths (and sometimes also within the same faith) do have distinctive and differing perspectives on truth may be liberating. For some, however, such an approach raises the potentially destabilising fear that truth is not absolute but relative. The secular institutions within which many chaplains work may be tempted, on the basis of commitment to equality, to present all truths as equally true, and thus by definition equally untrue.[3] Multi-faith chaplaincy challenges, and is challenged by, such narrow or absolutist theologies of truth.

The 'availability to all faiths and none' approach to chaplaincy effectively requires openness to the idea that 'truth' is not the exclusive property of one faith, or of one tradition within one faith: it is the job of chaplaincy and of chaplains to encourage a more nuanced understanding of what truth is, how and where and to whom it is revealed. This may be particularly necessary in the face of increasingly aggressive attempts from within a range of traditions, including some branches of Christianity, to impose one version of truth as 'more true' than others. To hold to such a nuanced understanding may perhaps limit the range of people who will be drawn to use the chaplaincy. But failure to do so may restrict the chaplain's ability to exercise ministry effectively within the parameters of an institution which demands the 'all faiths and none' approach. This presents the chaplain with a potential dilemma. Despite this, many chaplains do see it as an appropriate part of their role to promote an open and questioning approach to the identity and activity of God, which in turn enables a more open stance towards the Other.

I would want to suggest, therefore, that it is possible for Christians to work across faith boundaries without betraying the greater Truth to which we are committed, while respecting the commitment of colleagues from other traditions to the truth as it has been revealed to them. I believe that it is indeed possible to honour otherness and enter into shared awareness of the sacred without colluding with views which,

---

3   'Professional role requirements, encompassing an operational sense of "the spiritual", are held in tension with prior theological commitments and associated understandings of how faith space might operate' (Hewson and Crompton 2015, p.131).

as Christians, we cannot hold with integrity. The theological challenge facing Christian chaplains in multi-faith teams is not inconsiderable, but at a time when stridently exclusive versions of truth threaten to dominate any discussion of what it might mean to be 'religious', I would argue that there is an urgent need for Christian chaplains to model what might be termed 'generous orthodoxy' in this respect. This is certainly not to be understood as downplaying the distinctive truth claims of the Christian faith within the multi-faith context. Still less is it a call for religious relativism, but rather for a Christianity confident enough in its own perception of revealed truth not to fear *engagement* with those whose perceptions differ and for that engagement, where appropriate, to include the opportunity for shared worship.

My own calling as a Christian priest is shaped by my conviction that God is indeed true, but also that *Christianity* is true. Praying in silence together to the mysterious and unknowable God cannot express the *whole* truth of God's identity for Christians. Jesus Christ is 'the image of the invisible God' (Colossians 1.15), fully divine and fully human, and in him we are offered a unique solution to the question of whether or how we can know God. That perspective, which inescapably shapes my own perception of divine truth, presents an immediate and obvious problem for multi-faith working. It is my responsibility as an ordained minister of the Church to live out in a visible way my conviction that Christianity is true. At the same time, I am required by the institution in which I minister to work as an equal alongside colleagues who share my conviction that *God* is indeed true, but some of whose other beliefs I cannot share with integrity, any more than they can share mine.

Richard Sudworth describes this dilemma from an evangelical perspective. His Birmingham parish, set in a pre-dominantly Muslim area, welcomed Muslim families to a children's club hosted in the church building. The theological perspective of the parish was one in which conversion, and the primacy of Christianity over other perspectives, was intrinsic to their identity. But Sudworth came to question this as a motive for service: 'Are we seeing Muslims for who they are, in all their fullness, or as recipients for what we want to do to them?' In a sense, then, what Sudworth describes as the 'integral mission' of a Christian-led community project arguably demonstrates a Catholic ecclesiology, in that the very identity and function of an Anglican parish is fulfilled through becoming 'a safe space to all faiths and none' within its community (Sudworth 2011, pp.189–202).

Incarnation, representation and identity

'Doing Christology' is more problematic in the multi-faith environment than the exploration of different theologies. The 'otherness' of different traditions is not of the same order as the otherness of God. God is not 'like', not classifiable in terms of anything or anyone, but of an entirely different nature and being from anything else that is. For those within the Christian tradition, something of the nature of God is nonetheless revealed in the incarnate Christ. Therefore, the distinctiveness or otherwise of Christ is clearly a key issue for multi-faith working: Jesus' statement 'No one comes to the Father except through me' (John 14.6) can be used (by either 'side') to close down dialogue completely. Karl Rahner, Jesuit theologian, coined the phrase 'anonymous Christian' to include those who live good lives according to their own faith or ethical code; he argued that they honour God by living with integrity according to their own value systems, and will therefore be saved (McCool 1975). This description is problematic, in as much as many of those included within the 'anonymous Christian' category would actively object to being so described.

Chaplains of *every* faith, denomination and perspective need to stand as in some way representative of their respective communities, but the ways in which that is lived out in reality will vary widely. The assertion that the purpose of human beings, as understood by Christian theology, is to grow more fully into the divine image which we were created to reflect, forces us to confront the theological implications of representation in chaplaincy. Christian chaplains in some sense understand themselves as *in persona Christi*, an embodiment of an incarnational or sacramental presence. While chaplains of other faiths are clearly unable to use such language about their own representative role and may even find it offensive, they can and do witness to God's presence and activity within a secular institution in ways consonant with their own traditions. The representative role of non-Christian chaplains therefore raises questions not merely about different forms of external relationship and validation from within their particular faith community, but about how the different faiths' understandings of truth and of God can be honoured.

The precise representative function of humanist or atheist 'chaplains' is harder to define (see Ryan 2015, p.11). In so far as it has been developed at all, it tends to focus on function (for example, the provision of non-religious funerals or naming ceremonies) rather than on the question of representation. Yet the rejection of an instrumentalist view of education, healthcare or the penal system is by no means restricted solely to people of faith, and the wider discussion of human worth and purpose enabled by chaplains to secular institutions can usefully include non-religious perspectives.

Christian chaplaincy is frequently described in terms of 'incarnational presence'. That being the case, Christian chaplains are called to be 'doers', or perhaps more precisely 'embodiers' of the Word (James 1.12). The difficulty of defining or quantifying what it is that chaplains *do* has contributed to the attitude in some parts of the Church that this is not 'proper' ministry, in contrast to the parochial model, and in secular institutions that it is an unaffordable luxury.[4]

---

4   Threlfall-Holmes and Newitt (2011) offer a number of useful reflections on the range of tasks, roles and models of chaplaincy across different sectors.

However, there is a growing understanding, both across and beyond religious traditions, that chaplaincy might indeed be about presence: not so much in the incarnational sense as discussed above, but more literally, being present in time of need. The value of accompanying another human being at key moments of transition, need or vulnerability is not necessarily easy to quantify, but it is essential to both the task and the nature of chaplaincy. Clearly, Christian models of personhood do not translate appropriately to other faiths because they are rooted in the concept of relationship between divinity and humanity as embodied in Jesus Christ; but all faiths and spiritual paths have a shared interest in how faith speaks to the human condition and the quest for personhood. The chaplains, of whatever faith, may be the only people within an institution whose entire role centres on that question, as opposed to an instrumental function.

Understood in this way, some of the questions about how non-Christian faiths relate to models of chaplaincy formed out of Christian conceptions of truth begin to resolve themselves. An imam, for example, is not clericalised or sacramentalised in the same way as a Christian priest, and their presence is emphatically not understood as iconic in the way that a Christian priest might be thought to be *in persona Christi*. The way a Muslim chaplain lives out the relationship between representation and function is therefore different from that of a Christian, but it enables the expression of particular religious and spiritual needs, and gives the Muslim community a voice in negotiations with an institution or a sector should it be required (Gilliat-Ray *et al.* 2013, p.11).

Ecclesiology and religious literacy

For the Christian, particularly the Catholic Christian, questions of identity and belonging are inevitably bound up with the identity of the Church. What does it mean for chaplains to represent the Church in their context? The conventional understanding of Anglican chaplaincy, at least, was that it extended the ministry of the parish church into secular environments (Todd 2011, p.89). This will no longer do. Chaplaincy operates within an increasing recognition and acceptance that pluralism is the norm and that Christianity, let alone Anglican Christianity, is no longer the default setting in society.[5] Yet, despite evidence of a weakening in denominational affiliation among the Christian population, there is a growing awareness that broader religious identity does matter, in that it shapes and informs belonging. The research of Guest *et al.* into student Christianity (2013) suggests that traditional denominational loyalties are largely irrelevant: church affiliation is driven less by particular understandings of doctrine or practice than congenial worship or feeling accepted. Roman Catholic students proved an exception, though their strong denominational identity was arguably more cultural than doctrinal.

The very fact that chaplains are supplied by the Church or other faith groups to serve in a particular institution demonstrates their endorsement of that institution's purpose, while simultaneously allowing a space for questioning or critique from a faith perspective (Clines 2008, p.39). Chaplaincy's continued presence in secular institutions challenges, implicitly or otherwise, any attempt to reduce their identity and purpose to a row of numbers on a balance sheet; it enables the articulation of a holistic vision in which people are not treated primarily as economic units. While it is obviously impossible for non-Christian chaplains to agree that the ultimate purpose of humanity is to grow into the likeness of Christ, the rejection by all faiths of reductive secular instrumentalism may still create common ground around which chaplains of differing faiths can shape a discussion of purpose and meaning. Heap (2012)

---

5   A YouGov survey in January 2016 found that 46 per cent of the adult population of the UK identified as belonging to 'no religion'.

draws on Newman's *Idea of a University*, which describes the purpose of a university as a place of Christian formation. Similarly, the NHS charter enshrines spiritual and religious care within a holistic understanding of medicine (Lie 2001, p.184). Chaplaincy's continued presence in such institutions challenges reductive understandings of humanity.

The provision of appropriate faith support is now enshrined within human rights legislation, religion or belief being a protected characteristic under the 2010 Equality Act, and should therefore be reflected in the equality policies of institutions that have chaplains. The same equality policies can place pressure on chaplains to work equally with 'all faiths and none' in ways which they may not be fully equipped to do. Secular institutions are beginning to recognise the need to develop a degree of religious literacy in order to understand the nuanced boundaries of identity within faith groups, and avoid the inappropriate appointment of chaplains who will not be accepted as representative of 'their' community.[6]

Yet just as chaplains are called to critique or support the purpose of their host institution from a faith perspective, so too may they feel called to critique or support the Church from the perspective of those among whom they minister. If they represent the presence of God to their environment, so too do they represent institutional religion through an ecclesiology of presence. This is not always an easy balance to keep, but chaplains have an important role to play in promoting religious literacy at the institutional as well as the personal level. In a climate which assumes that secularism is neutral, it is easy to question whether the representatives of specific religious traditions have anything meaningful to contribute to the life of a secular institution. Without that embedded religious

---

6   Ryan (2015, p.24ff) examines in some detail the range of faiths and denominations working in some form of chaplaincy in Luton. He also highlights that some institutions did not know what branch of Islam, Christianity or Judaism their chaplains represented, and that some chaplains were being burdened with the expectation that their status as 'religious professionals' would equip them to act as experts on all religious traditions, including those other than their own.

identity, rooted in both belief and practice and connected in some way to the living, worshipping community of the Church, there can be no real engagement with the questions which religion poses to the secular narrative.

Trinitarian truth and perichoretic teams

One of the most contentious issues in chaplaincy is the fact that until relatively recently, there has been an assumption that the lead or coordinating chaplain in a multi-faith team will be an Anglican. In prisons, where chaplaincy has a statutory role, this may be seen as a relatively neutral function of the fact that the Church of England is the state church (Gilliat-Ray *et al.* 2013, p.5; Ryan 2015, p.62). The fact that the state church has a presence (however contested) in the public square may even be seen as an advantage for all faith communities, not just its own, in that it challenges the view that secularism is a neutral position (Ryan 2015, pp.56–57). I would argue that Anglicanism's clear vocation to provide a cure of souls to all, not just its own members, still equips it well to work within the demands of an 'all faiths and none' approach to chaplaincy. The 'polity of presence' in every community, a pastoral availability to those of any faith and no faith who choose to use it, is uniquely part of the DNA of Anglicanism (Quash 2003).

However, chaplains of other faiths have raised concerns that the largely unchallenged centrality of the Anglican model makes recruitment of chaplains more difficult, particularly to senior roles. It may also shape praxis in a particular direction, which arguably lessens distinctiveness (Lie 2001, p.189). The Anglican assumption of 'patronage and oversight' is increasingly critiqued as a historic anomaly, and some chaplains of other faith traditions have voiced a fear of being dominated by 'Anglican imperialism' (Lie 2001, p.190; Ryan 2015, p.11). As society continues to evolve, we can probably expect the number of those who identify as belonging to 'no faith' to increase yet further, in which case *any* faith perspective, including that of Anglican Christianity, will find itself in a position of minority. The effect on multi-faith chaplaincy team cohesion could potentially be a positive *if* it equalises the power imbalances inherent in unequal funding and resourcing of chaplaincy.

One way to redress such a perceived imbalance might be through the development of a theology of team rooted in the Trinity. The relationship between the Persons of the Trinity is often described using the term *perichoresis*, implying something dynamic and non-hierarchical, which could provide a healthier and more open model of team working than one in which any one faith or tradition assumes the right to lead. Although obviously derived from an explicitly Christian model, the concept of *perichoresis* emphasises the inherently relational character of teamwork, and challenges expectations about patterns of leadership and power in a way that can potentially enable all to participate as equals, whatever their background. Lie (2001, p.187ff), however, rightly questions whether the use of Christian terminology compromises the way other faiths approach chaplaincy. When even alternative descriptions of the key tasks of chaplaincy, such as 'pastoral care', are themselves derived from Judaeo-Christian language, other faiths may struggle to participate fully in an understanding of the role shaped by that language.

There are clearly limits to the extent to which Trinitarian *perichoresis* can work as an analogy for teamwork, because it so easily slips into modalism. Inasmuch as 'the chaplaincy' speaks or acts unanimously, it can model 'unity in diversity' to a certain extent, but there is a necessary separation or distinctiveness between the constituent parts, and a range of roles and functions shared out between the team members, none of which can be true of the Trinity. At the same time, the strength of the perichoretic image of leadership is in its non-hierarchical dynamism, the seamless mutuality of recognition and authority that allows one to speak for the whole without being perceived as inappropriately controlling or assuming a position of superiority. In the healthy perichoretic team, differing strengths, relationships and experience can be expressed as each member is trusted to take the lead in a given situation, or becomes the 'face of chaplaincy' on a particular committee, or speaks out on behalf of the rest on a contentious issue – but is equally trusted to relinquish leadership to another member of the team in dealing with a different scenario. The internal dynamic of perichoretic team relationships thus ensures that the chaplaincy team does not relate in a static or one-dimensional way to those outside it. There are practical difficulties with the execution of this model, but its absolute reliance on effective communication, openness to and acceptance of each other as equals, is, however imperfectly, a reflection of the relationships within the Godhead.

In arguing for a model of chaplaincy which rejects the generic and celebrates the riches of distinctive faith traditions, Pattison makes it possible to argue for a Trinitarian, perichoretic model of team that is genuinely 'creative and non-oppressive' to those of other faiths (Pattison 2001, p.45). If it is a step too far to claim the role of co-ordinating chaplain for the Spirit, perhaps it is not too fanciful to imagine a team in which the Spirit animates dynamic equality across traditions. The best multi-faith chaplaincy teams mirror our common experience of the divine, in so far as the dialogue that takes place between team members mirrors the internal dynamism of the Trinity – a dialogue that is active, not passive, relational, not defensive and is an ongoing conversation which has encounter with and intimate recognition of the Other at its heart.

What makes space sacred?

Another difficult practical issue for multi-faith chaplaincy is the negotiation of shared space. Institutional policies on the management of multi-faith space will not necessarily be formulated with much awareness of theological con-siderations, but will need to be worked out in theological terms by those whose responsibility includes religious and spiritual care.[7]

Use of space is informed by the nature of our engagement with the search for truth. Does the ordering of sacred space within an institution, and the arrangements made for meeting, catering or worshiping within that space, speak of one God (albeit open to varied understandings and interpretations) or of entirely separate paths which preclude any meaningful encounter? Lie (2001, p.189), for example, argues that the provision of a multi-faith room and a Christian chapel in the same institution implies that Christianity is not included within a multi-faith approach but regards itself, or is regarded, as distinct from it.

In a secular institution driven by function, result or achievement, the provision of any designated space for *being*, as opposed to *doing*, may be all the more important. But that very breadth of approach raises the question of how to ensure that a space within a secular institution is truly open to use by all the members of that institution, of every possible shade of belief and opinion. What speaks to one group of the numinous may look to another like irreverence or idolatry. The risk is that in order to be usable on an equal footing by all faiths and none, such a space will necessarily be so bland and empty of symbolism that it does not speak in any way of God, mystery or transcendence, so it is hard to see how such a space can be understood as truly sacred. Crompton (2013, pp.474–96) argues while the aim of designers is to create a space that is genuinely open and inclusive to all, and to prevent their taking on a symbolism which is 'meaningful in an inappropriate way', the result may be a mundane 'empty white room', whose lack of features precludes a sense of the numinous.

In the light of current questions about no platforming in various areas of public life, there may be a tendency to play safe

---

7   *AMOSSHE Insight: Multi-faith space on campus* (Simon Lee, Northumbria University 2015) attempts to create a 'positive' approach to multi-faith spaces in response to the 'negative' perception of Crompton (2013).

by not confronting difficult or divisive questions. However neutral their appearance, spaces set aside for encounter with the divine in any form are not necessarily the same as 'safe spaces' within which it is impossible to express anything that offends the other. A multi-faith space worthy of the name can never be entirely safe, in the sense that it makes no room for disagreement or conflict: discussion of contentious issues is necessary for mutual understanding. There is a clear role for chaplaincy in framing such discussion or debate on behalf of the institution or organisation in which it is set. Chaplains provide space within which all are confronted with what it is like to *be* 'other', uncomfortable though that is, through being confronted with the ultimate Otherness of God. One of the increasingly important aspects of multi-faith chaplaincy is to model such encounters, and to provide access to the possibility of meeting otherness in a non-threatening environment where difference is held and difficult voices are heard, but in a way which enables all to participate as equals.

Conclusion

As we have seen, there is an increasingly individualised, consumerist slant to religious identity, which poses a considerable challenge to chaplaincy's understanding of its own purpose. There is also a recognised need to respond flexibly to those whose search for meaning and purpose is not located within organised religion but 'in the interstices of the patchwork of faiths and beliefs to be found in contemporary society' (Todd 2011, p.90). A detailed discussion of generic or interfaith chaplaincy lies beyond the scope of this chapter. It suffices to say here that, done badly or with inadequate religious literacy, generic chaplaincy is 'a failure of authenticity', diluting what is distinctive and valuable in every faith tradition.[8]

---

8   Clines 2008, p.14; Pattison (2001, p.34) refers to generic chaplaincy damningly as 'metaphysical marshmallow'.

A sense of being firmly rooted in one's own faith tradition may give chaplains of any background the confidence to engage in genuine dialogue beyond it. Working together, not despite but through the reality of religious difference, can demonstrate something powerful to an otherwise sceptical institution. A healthy, genuinely multi-faith chaplaincy team both demonstrates the ability to draw together around the shared identity of faith, and enables the distinctive expressions of different faiths.

Above all, the multi-faith chaplaincy has an important role in promoting and modelling dialogue which does not airbrush out important areas of difference, but demonstrates a willingness to work together through the pain of disunity. The refusal to fear complexity or disagreement is vital for mature multi-faith working, whether within teams or at the institutional level. 'Good disagreement' is not just a pious aspiration, but is something which a multi-faith chaplaincy team can model to both their host institution and their constituent faith groups.

The whole range of faiths represented in a team can unite around their shared commitment to truth. There will inevitably be differences in how truth is understood, experienced and lived by representatives of different faiths; but their shared insistence that the search for truth can be, and should be, located within a religious worldview is an important corrective to the instrumental secularism which drives so many of the institutions which host chaplaincy.

References

Clines, J. (2008) *Faiths in Higher Education Chaplaincy*. Church of England Board of Education.

Crompton, A. (2013) 'The architecture of multifaith spaces: God leaves the building.' *Journal of Architecture 18* (4), 474–96.

Faith and Order Commission (2016) *Communion and Disagreement* (GS Misc 1139, Archbishops' Council 2016).

Gilliat-Ray, S., Ali, M. and Pattison, S. (2013) *Understanding Muslim Chaplaincy*. Aldershot: Ashgate.

Gilliat-Ray, S. and Arshad, M. (2015) 'Multi-Faith Working.' In C. Swift, M. Cobb and A. Todd *A Handbook of Chaplaincy Studies: Understanding Spiritual Care in Public Places*. Aldershot: Ashgate.

Guest, M., Aune, K., Sharma, S. and Warner R. (2013) *Christianity and the University Experience: Understanding Student Faith*. London: Bloomsbury.

Harris S. (2014) *Waking Up: A Guide to Spirituality Without Religion*. New York: Simon and Schuster.

Heap, S. (2012) *What are Universities Good For?* Cambridge: Grove Books.

Hewson, C. and Crompton, A. (2015) 'Managing Multi-Faith Spaces: the Chaplain as Entrepreneur.' In C. Swift, M. Cobb and A. Todd *A Handbook of Chaplaincy Studies: Understanding Spiritual Care in Public Places*. Aldershot: Ashgate.

Lee, S. (2015) AMOSSHE Insight: Multi-faith space on campus. Accessed on 7/7/2017 at: www.amosshe.org.uk/insight-2014-15-multi-faith-space.

Legood, G. (1999) *Chaplaincy: The Church's Sector Ministries*. London: Cassell.

Lie, A. (2001) 'No Level Playing Field: The Multi-Faith Context and its Challenges.' In H. Orchard (ed.) *Spirituality in Healthcare Contexts*. London: Jessica Kingsley Publishers.

Lipner, J. (1994) *Hindus: Their Religious Beliefs and Practices*. London: Routledge.

McCool, G.A (ed.) (1975) *A Rahner Reader*. London: Darton, Longman and Todd.

Newman, J. H. (1996) 'The Idea of a University.' In F.M. Turner (ed.) *The Idea of a University*. New Haven: Yale University Press.

Pattison, S. (2001) 'Dumbing Down the Spirit.' In H. Orchard (ed.) *Spirituality in Healthcare Contexts*. London: Jessica Kingsley Publishers.

Quash, B. (2003) 'The Anglican Church as a Polity of Presence.' In D. Dormor, J. McDonald and J. Caddick (eds) *Anglicanism: The Answer to Modernity*. London: Continuum.

Ryan, B. (2015) *A Very Modern Ministry: Chaplaincy in the UK*. London: Theos.

Slater, V. (2015) *Chaplaincy Ministry and the Mission of the Church*. London: SCM Press.

Sudworth, R. (2011) 'Holistic Responses in Multicultural Birmingham.' In C. Chapman and S. Bell (eds) *Between Naivety and Hostility: Uncovering the Best Christian Responses to Islam in Britain*. London: Authentic Media.

Threlfall-Holmes, M. and Newitt M. (eds) (2011) *Being a Chaplain*. London: SPCK.

Todd, A. (2011). 'Responding to Diversity: Chaplaincy in a Multi-faith Context.' In M. Threlfall-Holmes and M. Newitt (eds) *Being a Chaplain*. London: SPCK.

4

THEOLOGY AND MODELS OF CHAPLAINCY

BEN RYAN

Introduction

In one sense, there is nothing new about chaplaincy. There have been chaplains for a very long time in various institutional settings, notably hospitals, the military, universities and prisons. What is new is the sense of chaplaincy as a phenomenon which is on the rise, with a remarkable spread into ever new areas of British public life.

Chaplaincy has become extraordinarily broad and difficult to easily pigeon-hole. How can a single model encompass at once a full-time Anglican vicar living alongside soldiers on campaign with that of a lay volunteer visiting a shopping centre? These contexts, and the work being done within them, share a title 'chaplaincy' but are too disparate to provide clear 'one size fits all' models.

Yet there are some uniting features to this spread. One is that chaplains are public operators. Their role is going out to where people are, as opposed to waiting for people to come to faith groups, and confronting society as it is, rather than as faith groups might want it to be. That being the case, there ought to be some unifying theology that can group together the nature of this public-facing religious work – even if the contexts in which it is employed remain remarkably disparate.

There is a range of available models for chaplaincy on which such a theology might hang. The unifying feature of good chaplaincy models, this chapter argues, is one of personalism – an attitude that speaks to humanity's innate need for relationships (both between individual people and between individuals and God) in fulfilling our individual nature.

I shall begin by considering four themes that define the changing nature of chaplaincy models before looking at a set of possible models, both theological and secular, that have been applied to chaplaincy.

Themes creating change in chaplaincy models

In looking at models for chaplaincy there are a number of developing overall themes that are worth considering. Not all are equally relevant (or even present at all) in every chaplaincy setting, but these themes do set the scene for some of the ways in which models are changing.

The role of the chaplain has evolved over time in line with the evolving religious and social landscape

Most Christian chaplaincy throughout the twentieth century operated effectively as an extension of the parish model. The sorts of service, religious and pastoral, usually provided within a parish were taken to those who for whatever reason were unable to attend their parish church (perhaps due to incarceration, military service, hospitalisation or being away at boarding school or university). This functioned within a context in which for most of the century society was unquestionably Christian. It was, therefore, entirely uncontroversial that the 1952 Prisons Act specifies only three compulsory prison staff: 'a governor, a chaplain and a medical officer' (Her Majesty's Government 1952).

Today the social context in which chaplaincy is operating has changed dramatically. According to the 2011 Census 59 per cent of the UK call themselves Christian (down from 72 per cent a decade earlier), 11 per cent belong to a different religion and 25 per cent have no religion (Office for National Statistics 2012). The British Social Attitudes survey of 2014 shows that just 18 per cent of the British call themselves Anglican, and 8 per cent Catholic. There has been a significant growth both in raw numbers and in public awareness of minority faiths, particularly Islam, and among those of no religion.

With these changes the assumptions underpinning public life have shifted. The primary space for religious engagement has shifted; today, encounter with religion is less likely than ever before to take place within a parish church. Chaplaincy, accordingly, is no longer an *ancillary* service that extended the core business of the parish to those outside a normal parish context, but is now increasingly becoming a *primary* meeting point between religion and society (Ryan 2015, p.79).

Chaplaincy has proved particularly suited to such a change in context and as a result it is no surprise to see chaplaincy expanding from its traditional settings into an ever-broader space including sports clubs, town centres and workplaces (Ryan 2015, pp.14–16). Partly this is because of the nature of chaplaincy. The British may no longer be going to church, but they are certainly going to continue going to work, to hospital and into other public spaces. The great advantage of chaplaincy versus other forms of Christian ministry is that it is innately public. Chaplains are always operating outside a church context – they are going to where people already actually sit.

There is a wider sense of the appropriateness of chaplaincy to the modern world. In a society which is ever more mobile and individualised, chaplaincy retains an appeal by being present in often very personal relationships with service users in their own unique context (such as the workplace).

The personal connection is hugely important in countering the idea of religion as an old-fashioned structure alien to the lives of most people. It appeals in that sense to what Grace Davie famously identified as the persistent sense of 'vicarious religion' (Davie 1994) – the appeal of some sort of latent religious sensitivity without much active churchgoing.

Chaplaincy as a necessarily bilingual ministry

Connected to the changing landscape is the theme that chaplaincy models will need to take full account of the need to be 'bilingual' – speaking the language both of religious ministry and the context-specific language of their setting. A prison chaplain, for example, must be able to speak in religious terms of the point and nature of their work, but also to do the same in the official public language of the prison service.

In line with the way the overall context has changed we should be conscious that it is no longer taken for granted that religion has a place in public spaces. Though England maintains an Established Church, in practice most public spaces have an assumed secularism. The case for chaplaincy needs to be made at least in part on terms that demonstrate its utility in the public language of the different settings. The 'secular' models discussed below take on a particular significance here.

The end of clerical chaplaincy?

A third theme changing the models of chaplaincy is the increasing move away from chaplaincy being the exclusive activity of clergy. Of course, in many Christian denominations and non-Christian religions there are no clergy anyway, or at least a very different conception of the role. However, even among Anglican and Catholic chaplaincies that have historically been largely the remit of clergy there has been a noticeable shift.

Partly this can be tied to the fact that the role in many sectors is now becoming more part-time and volunteer-led. A case study undertaken by Theos (Ryan 2015, p.27) in Luton found 169 chaplains of whom only 39 had received some sort of religious training (such as that leading to ordination). Clear national data is hard to find on this. Analysis of official returns from Anglican dioceses showed 1321 ordained chaplains and only 248 lay chaplains (Todd, Slater and Dunlop 2014). However, that report concluded that there was a significant gap in data held on lay roles. The authors suggested that while that data put the ratio at 8:1 ordained to lay, in all likelihood it was closer to the other way round in reality.

Despite this shift, it is fair to say that much of the focus, particularly in finding a model of ministry or theology, remains premised on the assumption that the chaplain is likely to be an ordained minister. It is notable how much pastoral theology work continues to hark back to Gregory the Great's sixth-century 'Pastoral Rule' – a book designed as advice to a newly appointed bishop. Even today the development of practical theology often retains a tension over the exact breakdown of such roles to be particularly considered clerical and those which are to be entrusted to the laity. Benedict XVI's *Deus Caritas Est* (2005) is typical of the trend, stressing the character of the Church in providing a threefold ministry: proclaiming the word of God, celebrating the sacraments and exercising charity. Yet which of these, if any, are to be done by the laity is left noticeably unclear.

This raises some particular challenges for modern-day models. For example, if part of the role of chaplaincy is to deliver religious services, there are particular aspects that are currently reserved for ordained clergy. For example, only Catholic priests may hear confession, or say Mass, so if Catholic chaplaincy roles are going to be filled by the laity, that raises a challenge.

The intended beneficiaries

The intended beneficiaries of chaplaincy were once obvious. The great majority of the population were practising Anglicans and Anglican chaplains ministered to them while Roman Catholics, Methodists and others provided chaplains to support their own denominations. That model fits awkwardly into today's more diverse Britain. Chaplains in most fields are expected to minister to anyone, regardless of faith or belief. This is made explicit in many codes of conduct and contracts (see, for example, the UK Board of Healthcare Chaplaincy's Code of Conduct for Healthcare Chaplains).

Yet this is not always an entirely clear distinction, certainly not in the case of the many unpaid visitor and volunteer chaplaincy roles. Plenty of chaplains are appointed precisely due to the desire to have a representative of a particular faith group. There is a difference in model between those chaplains (usually volunteers or sessional appointments) who are called in when requested by a member of their faith group, and those in more regular capacities who are more embedded in the everyday life of their setting.

This difference has consequences. One is a fear of imperialism – of Anglicans being assumed (by virtue of their Established Church model) to be able to speak to anyone, and therefore, for them to disproportionately dominate the paid and leadership roles within chaplaincy teams. This can cause resentment among other chaplains who feel sidelined. It is also a legitimate concern that there can be an assumption that one chaplain is as good as any other, whereas several pieces of research have suggested that service users prefer chaplains of their own faith and do not always feel sufficiently catered for by others (Orchard 2000; Siddiqui 2007).

Models of chaplaincy

The four themes above each provide important context in which chaplaincy models are developing. In terms of the specific theological and secular models on which chaplaincy can draw, a good summary was provided by Miranda Threlfall-Holmes in *Being a Chaplain* (Threlfall-Holmes and Newitt 2011). Her schema split chaplaincy models between theological and secular:

Theological

- missionary
- pastor
- historical/parish model
- agent of challenge
- incarnational/sacramental.

Secular

- pastoral care
- spiritual care
- diversity model
- tradition/heritage model
- specialist service provider.

My intention is to build on those same models while adding to the theological models the ideas of 'cultist' and 'exile', and to the secular models a 'community mediator' model. It should be noted that few if any chaplains will fall only within one model – they are necessarily interacting with one another, not least given the theme of bilingualism highlighted above. The strongest theological models are those that are most mindful of the power of relationships and encounter, and several of the models presented below need some adjustment to better reflect that point.

Theological chaplaincy models

Missionary

In the context of an increasingly secular society the appeal of a missionary model is obvious. It has in it that sense of going out and taking the gospel to the unchurched. This is also a model which suits the issue of chaplaincy having to fit into very different contexts – finding language to suit the particular situation of, for example, a prison.

The danger of the missionary model lies in chaplains being perceived as agents of 'proselytism' – using a position to abuse vulnerable people, or otherwise seeming inappropriate within a plural and multi-faith space (Bickley 2015). It is also something which seems to be more openly discussed in some sectors than others. Town-centre chaplains and sports chaplains are almost universally Christian (versus the more diverse NHS and prison sectors, for example) and often drawn from more openly evangelical Christian traditions. They are correspondingly more likely to talk in terms of mission and evangelism, than say, NHS chaplains, who seem more wary of the charge of inappropriate behaviour in the public square. Nor is such reticence entirely due to a concern to be seen to be acceptable to secular employers. More generally there seems to be a conscious desire to avoid being an evangelist among many chaplains.

If chaplains are barred from evangelising by secular spaces and therefore refrain from seeing themselves as missionaries, there is a possible tension between the theological basis of chaplaincy and what they are doing in practice. If, however, their reticence is about something more than official policy, that raises a more challenging theological question as to whether evangelism is viewed as a genuine part of ministry by chaplains. To put it another way, are chaplains scared of the possibility of evangelism?

It is worth noting that the missionary model does not necessarily mean explicit 'proselytising' activity. A common line from chaplains in interviews for the Theos project was the quote attributed to St Francis that they sought 'to preach the gospel. If necessary, use words.' This sense of being a witness to faith without being 'preachy', as many phrased it, has a strong theological pedigree within this missionary model.

Threlfall-Holmes includes this as the first of the theological models, and yet it seems to be one of the most contested by chaplains themselves. There is understandable concern to avoid what Pope Francis has called 'the solemn nonsense' of proselytism: crude, unsubtle, even rude attempts to convince others of the truth of Christianity. Those are fair concerns, but there is also a need to be mindful that mission is a fundamental tenet of Christianity, and that going out and spreading the gospel, whether via words or deeds, is a part of Christian ministry.

In some of the models that follow the power of chaplaincy as encounter is discussed. This is also a key point for the missionary model. Chaplaincy work at its heart is about encounters between chaplain and service user, where the chaplain is manifesting in that relationship something of God's love for humanity. There is power in such encounters, with at least the potential for radical transformation in the life of the service user. The missionary model, like several of the models below, is at its best about the power of relationships to create change.

Pastor

If the missionary model feels as if it particularly gets at the idea of being a public ministry in a space with many non-Christians, then the pastor model provides a specific focus on the caring content of the ministry.

Like the missionary model, it is about witnessing to the love of God through service to others. It is in some ways the easiest theological model to sell to secular spaces, since it ties closely to secular models of spiritual and pastoral care. The output amounts to the same (pastoral care), the difference is in the theological background. So, for example, in Winnifred Fallers Sullivan's book, *A Ministry of Presence* (Fallers Sullivan 2014, p.178), the idea of presence in chaplaincy is tied in with the idea of servanthood (*diakonia*).

The question in this model is whether there is sufficient theological content for it to be durable in its own right. Certainly, there is a biblical case to be made for the necessity of caring for the vulnerable, with the parables of the good Samaritan (Luke 10.25–37) and the parable of the sheep and goats (Matthew 25.31–46) being just two frequently quoted examples. There is little, however, distinctively Christian about most pastoral care. Christians are certainly called to care for the vulnerable, but as a model for chaplaincy, simply caring for others is a rather limited vision of the role.

Historical/parish model

This model is essentially the original model of chaplaincy – an extension of the parish to those unable for whatever reason to attend a parish church. It works best within strong institutional settings with a clearly defined community. Military chaplains are a classic example of Christian ministers taking the parish model on military campaigns, but similar models exist within schools, prisons and universities.

In the university context, this brings up a philosophical split over chaplaincy models. Catholic students have been actively encouraged to view the university chaplaincy literally as their own parish, taking Mass and the other sacraments together with fellow students (Pontifical Council for the Pastoral Care of Migrants and Itinerant People 2004). Other Christian denominations have shied away from such a model, with chaplains encouraged to perform a more general role for the institution as a whole and/or to encourage Christians to attend local churches. For those latter chaplains, chaplaincy is not considered to be providing a church for worshippers within a place in the same way that Catholics might see it. It is interesting to note that research indicates that engagement with university chaplaincy by mainstream Protestants is significantly lower than it is among Catholic or Pentecostal students – perhaps indicating that engagement is higher among those groups that view chaplaincy more as a localised church (Aune 2016).

The broader question is whether such a model remains desirable. It certainly meets the particular needs of Christians within certain contexts (particularly those who are unable to attend a local church), but in other ways can be seen as promoting an insular vision of Christianity. Where chaplains' great advantage is their ability to go to people, rather than requiring people to come to church, this seems to perpetuate the struggles of the parish model.

Agent of challenge

In a number of chaplaincy models there is an idea of the chaplain as a figure able to challenge or confront behaviour within their setting. Most commonly this is associated with people using the language of 'prophet' in describing their role. This might involve challenging particular policies or practices within an organisation.

The gap between this and other theological models is that this role performs a very different function. The missionary, the pastor and the incarnational role (below) are all following established models of pastoral theology originally applied (at least primarily) to priests. Their target, in each case, is individuals within the space in which chaplains work – prisoners, employees, patients and so on. The prophet figure, by contrast, is speaking primarily to the institution. This function is about being a voice for justice, rather than care, challenging the practice of organisations, rather than simply working within them.

The focus of this model on justice makes it one of the few models that works particularly well for lay chaplains. Justice, in Catholic social teaching, has been considered as political work and, therefore, the priority of the laity. Celebrating the sacraments (as in a parish model), teaching or proclaiming the gospel (as in the missionary model) and pastoral care (as in the pastor model), by contrast, have been seen as duties belonging particularly to clergy. That distinction is less meaningful in other Christian theological traditions – but does at least serve to highlight that this model operates in quite a different theological register to other chaplaincy models.

Incarnational/sacramental

This model is similar to the missionary and pastor models in being tied up with the idea of substantiating the love of God or the message of the Christian faith within the person of the chaplain. The difference from the pastoral model is that if that model focuses particularly on the activity of a chaplain, this one has tended to focus on the simple fact of the chaplain's presence. Some prefer to use the language of sacrament – with chaplains by virtue of their existence in a place being a physical manifestation of God's love.

There are a number of potential problems with this model. One is translating it into any sense that is meaningful to secular spaces – where it can sound like special pleading and refusing to actually committing to really *do* anything! More fundamentally, the too frequently unacknowledged issue with this model is that it relies on the assumption that there actually is a regular chaplaincy presence. Increasingly, chaplaincy models are relying on part-time, volunteer and sessional services. Relatively few chaplains actually do constitute a constant real presence in the life of any given space, which for a model based on presence seems a fundamental weakness.

Nevertheless, this model gets towards the crux of chaplaincy. The weakness, as expressed in Threlfall-Holmes and elsewhere, is to focus this model too much on the identity of the chaplain, and too little on their methodology. Only a minority of chaplaincy work involves constant presence within a place (most chaplains are part time), but by contrast almost all chaplaincy work is involved in the business of relationships. The talk of sacramental presence makes the process sound too passive, unless it is understood within a context of deliberate relationship building.

This model might be stronger still, however, if it adapted the Catholic social teaching idea of 'personalism'. Personalism at its most basic is the idea that all humans are innately relational beings. It is based on Trinitarian theology, in which the three persons of the Trinity are essentially in relationship with one another. In the same way humans are understood not as atomised individuals, but as beings for whom maximising potential can only be done through relationships with others.

In this context, the point about incarnational theology is not simply that God became incarnate but that as God's incarnate, Jesus met, spoke to, healed and taught people. The fact of the incarnation is made more significant by the constant encounter between God and humanity in the life of Jesus. In the same way, chaplaincy's greatest theological tool is its ability to encounter people. To quote Pope Benedict XVI, 'Being Christian is not the result of an ethical choice or lofty idea but the encounter with an event, a person, which gives life a new horizon and decisive direction' (Benedict XVI 2005).

That encounter, in which the chaplain stands as the manifestation of God's love, even – perhaps especially – in places where hopelessness seems to dominate, is achieved through relationships. The matching together of a personalist sense of the importance of relationships alongside the idea of incarnation is the model of chaplaincy that seems most theologically robust, and true to what chaplains do in practice already.

To these theological models from Threlfall-Holmes there are two additional theological models (cultist and exile) proposed here to broaden the debate.

Cultist and/or exile?

Both these models revolve around a question of how integrated into the life of the wider Church chaplains really are. In the case of the former, the question is whether the people whom chaplains reach really get brought closer to the Church (or faith group) as a whole, or simply become a part of a smaller cult around the specific chaplaincy they have encountered. This is a danger highlighted by Stephen Pattison (Pattison 2015). He focuses on the changing trajectories of religion in Britain, with the decline in church attendance and the paradoxical growth in chaplaincy, and wonders whether this indicates that chaplaincy is itself becoming a religion – one which is quiescent to the multi-faith issues and professional agenda of the day and is utterly divorced from the wider Church.

If this seems a bit overstated it does nonetheless get at the fact that chaplains are often operating at something of a distance from the wider Church/faith/religion. Another aspect of that might be the idea of the chaplain as an exile – operating away from the Church. The difference between such a model and, say, the missionary model is that the latter is sent (literally the root *missio* being from the Latin to send or dispatch), with an implied connection back to the rest of the faith community, while an exile is separate (even deliberately detached) from that community. There is evidence to support the idea that a good proportion of chaplains feel actively disenfranchised from their Church. For example, a disproportionate number of Anglican chaplains are in same-sex partnerships, theologically liberal and likely to feel at odds with the Church, and therefore possibly using chaplaincy as an 'escape' from the Church (Swift 2014, p.157).

Both these models may have negative connotations, yet they are undoubtedly hinting at a real aspect of chaplaincy, and one that is dangerous for faith groups, who risk losing any benefit from their chaplains beyond their immediate context. It also represents a challenge for chaplains, for whom for whatever reason such a model may be attractive (as providing independence from difficult structures), but risks too great a detachment and loss of (at least potential) resources and support from the Church. At a theological level, the danger is in a breakdown of relationships.With the opening up of a world of transformative encounters, the risk is that if that world is too focused on a single chaplain, and not the wider church, then the service user will not be led any further on that potential journey.

Secular chaplaincy models

Aside from theological models, Threlfall-Holmes also lists a series of possible secular models. The interesting debate is how far these are compatible with the theological models. There should be a recognition that chaplaincy needs to be a bilingual operation – speaking the language of both faith and secular need. Critically, being bilingual needs authenticity. Institutions and organisations demand particular services of their chaplains, which form the basis for their invitation or payment. That is their prerogative and is not inherently problematic unless chaplains take those secular needs to be the only purpose of their work. That way lies the risk of the role becoming spiritually empty, devoid of genuine theological purpose or content.

For the purposes of this chapter, therefore, the models below are only considered in brief, and according to what consequences they might have for the theological models above.

Pastoral care

From a secular perspective, the ability of chaplains to provide pastoral care is often the key or even sole model that they support. What it means in practice is of course very broad and might vary markedly in different settings – producing very different output measures for chaplaincy.

The range is sufficiently wide to challenge the idea that this is a single model at all, but rather a catch-all term for the sort of work that characterises much of chaplaincy from a secular perspective. For chaplains, it carries with it a tension too, which is that if taken to the exclusion of all other models this relegates them to nothing more than being professional nice guys, or cheap welfare workers (Newitt 2011). The value theologically of this role is twofold. First, it coheres quite closely to the pastor model above; second, it opens up the space for relationships and encounters that, as argued above, are the key to understanding a theological model for chaplaincy.

Spiritual care

Unlike the pastoral care model, spiritual care assumes the importance of chaplains in meeting some sort of spiritual or religious need. For example, within the NHS context, an increasing focus is being placed on the contribution of chaplains to supporting spiritual health and wellbeing – with demonstrable effects on recovery, mental health and other factors (Kevern and Hill 2014; Raffay, Wood and Todd 2016).

Though these are secular models there is also a secular purpose in having a figure who particularly provides for religious needs that no other member of staff is suited to fulfil. For example, within the prison context, prisoners have the right to practise religion but obviously cannot leave the prison to attend a place of worship, nor would other prison staff be appropriate to run such activities.

Diversity model

The need for workplaces and public bodies to exhibit, support and promote diversity has led to both new chaplaincy models and challenges. Some chaplains (often titled something like 'interfaith advisers') have carved out a niche as diversity experts, working within organisations as advocates for minority religious groups and as advisers on policies – a role which seems to fit well with the theological role of prophet, even if it seems less applicable to other theological models, and less focused on relationships and encounters (Gilliat-Ray, Ali and Pattison 2013).

Tradition/heritage model

Chaplaincy is an old model of ministry and in many settings its sense of tradition or tie-in to the ethos and heritage of its context is essential to its appeal. This is particularly true in historic institutions with strong traditional identities, such as Oxbridge colleges, public schools and the military. The military makes for a specific case study, in which chaplains are part of the fabric of the institution, particularly surrounding key community bonding moments such as funerals and repatriations of service men and women killed abroad. Important as this role undoubtedly is in some contexts, it is probably fair to say that it has little theological content to it in most contexts.

Specialist service provider

Threlfall-Holmes uses this category as a meta-category to include a range of secular themes and models that use chaplaincy to meet some particular professional service – including the models used above or other common aspects of the role such as counselling or signposting to other services. For Threlfall-Holmes, a particular dimension of this is that this is a model that is demand-led – chaplains fulfil such services as users within a particular setting need and want. As such, we might conclude that this model particularly fits a new, more individualised secular society in which religion and spirituality are personal matters addressed according to a particular individual's need, rather than a more traditional society that might expect believers to go to a place of worship and accept a less personalised response.

More contentious is the role of chaplains in assisting with the Prevent agenda against extremism. This is particularly the case in prisons, but is also growing in school and university chaplaincy. What this means in practice varies from setting to setting, but certainly it would seem that there has been a significant amount of funding put towards Muslim prison chaplains in particular, fuelling a remarkable growth that now sees some 20 per cent of prison chaplains coming from that faith group, compared with 12 per cent of the prison population and 5 per cent of the general population (Todd 2011, p.95). This also adds a real danger, since potentially at least it creates a chaplaincy model in which chaplains are state agents employed with a particular counter-extremism role – a model which is very different from, and which risks undermining, other models (Todd 2013). Chaplaincy that rests on relationships needs trust to work. The perception that chaplains are there for security purposes is, to put it mildly, not conducive to trust. To these models we can add one additional model: the mediator and community bridge.

Mediator and community bridge

A final model of chaplaincy worth considering is the role of chaplains as community bridges. This role occurs in a number of settings. One is among police chaplains (particularly from minority faiths), who have a role not just in offering pastoral care to the police but also in helping them to make connections and grow relationships with local religious and ethnic minority communities. This role, as a bridge connecting one part of the community with another, perhaps more isolated or insular, part is replicated in other chaplaincies in different ways. Community chaplaincy, for example, works with ex-offenders, and several operate as charities both within and outside prisons, to help former prisoners rehabilitate into a waiting community, possibly via a local church or with a mentor.

Conclusions

This chapter has drawn attention to a number of developing themes within the chaplaincy world, and to several possible models. It is worth stressing again that not all of these themes and not all of the models will be equally relevant in every context. Chaplaincy is a field of immense breadth, and the difference between different settings makes it nearly impossible to find generally applicable themes.

Defining chaplaincy models outside the particular context of the chaplain in question is, as a result, something of a fool's errand, and this chapter has done no more than try at least to raise the parameters within which an evaluation might be made. Chaplains seeking a model might recall Paul VI's encyclical *Octogesima adveniens* which says of the Church's social teaching:

> If it does not intervene to authenticate a given structure or to propose a ready-made model, it does not thereby limit itself to recalling general principles. It develops through reflection applied to the changing situations of the world, under the driving force of the gospel as the source of renewal when its message is accepted in its totality and with all its demands. (Paul VI 1971)

Much the same could be said of chaplaincy; it need not have a ready-made model and certainly ought to reflect its particular context, yet it ought to recall also some specific theological principles that undergird it. Central to those principles is the critical nature of relationship building to chaplaincy. Several of the proposed models above, particularly the missionary and incarnational models, get at the crux of the issue but would be strengthened further if they included a more explicit concern for the essentially relational nature of humanity and the role of chaplains in creating transformational encounters. Chaplaincy across its various sectors is always at its best involved in the business of relationship building. That is often acknowledged, but sometimes insufficiently theologically grounded; what this chapter has attempted to do is to suggest ways in which that theological grounding might be clarified and strengthened.

References

Aune, K. (2016) Lecture in York in 2016, presenting research by Aune, K., Guest, M., Sharma, S. and Warner, R. Publication forthcoming.

Benedict XVI (2005) *Deus Caritas Est.* Vatican City: The Holy See. Accessed on 7/7/2017 at: http://w2.vatican.va/content/benedict-xvi/en/encyclicals/documents/hf_ben-xvi_enc_20051225_deus-caritas-est.html.

Bickley, P. (2015) *The Problem of Proselytism.* London: Theos.

Davie, G. (1994) *Religion in Britain Since 1945: Believing Without Belonging.* Oxford: Blackwell.

Fallers Sullivan, W. (2014) *A Ministry of Presence.* London: University of Chicago Press.

Gilliat-Ray, S., Ali, M. and Pattison, S. (2013) *Understanding Muslim Chaplaincy.* Aldershot: Ashgate.

Her Majesty's Government (1952) *The Prison Act.* London: HMSO. Accessed on 7/7/2017 at: www.legislation.gov.uk/ukpga/1952/52/pdfs/ukpga_19520052_en.pdf.

Kevern, P. and Hill, L. (2014) 'Chaplains for well-being in primary care: analysis of the results of a retrospective study.' *Primary Health Care Research & Development 16*(01): 1–13, January 2014.

Newitt, M. (2011) 'The Role and Skills of a Chaplain.' In M. Threlfall-Holmes and M. Newitt *Being a Chaplain.* London: SPCK.

Office for National Statistics (2012) *2011 Census Data.* London: ONS. Accessed on 7/7/2017 at: www.ons.gov.uk/peoplepopulationandcommunity/culturalidentity/religion/articles/religioninenglandandwales2011/2012-12-11.

Orchard, H. (2000) *Hospital Chaplaincy: Modern, Dependable?* Lincoln: Lincoln Theological Institute.

Pattison, S. (2015) 'Situating Chaplaincy in the United Kingdom: The Acceptable Face of 'Religion.' In C. Swift, M. Cobb and A. Todd *A Handbook of Chaplaincy Studies: Understanding Spiritual Care in Public Places.* Aldershot: Ashgate.

Paul VI (1971) *Octogesima adveniens.* Vatican City: The Holy See. Accessed on 7/7/2017 at: http://w2.vatican.va/content/paul-vi/en/apost_letters/documents/hf_p-vi_apl_19710514_octogesima-adveniens.html.

Pontifical Council for the Pastoral Care of Migrants and Itinerant People (2004) *Pastoral Care of Human Mobility in the Universities of Europe.* Vatican City: Pontifical Council for the Pastoral Care of Migrants and Itinerant People.

Raffay, J., Wood, E. and Todd, A. (2016) 'Service user views of spiritual and pastoral care (chaplaincy) in NHS mental health services: a co-produced constructivist grounded theory investigation.' *BMC Psychiatry* (2016) 16:200.

Ryan, B. (2015) *A Very Modern Ministry: Chaplaincy in the UK.* London: Theos.

Siddiqui, A. (2007) 'Islam at universities in England: meeting the needs and investing in the future.' *Islamic Studies 46:4* (Winter 2007), 559–570.

Swift, C. (2014) *Hospital Chaplaincy in the Twenty-First Century: The Crisis of Spiritual Care on the NHS.* 2nd Edition Aldershot: Ashgate.

Threlfall-Holmes, M. (2011) 'Exploring Models of Chaplaincy.' In M. Threlfall-Holmes and M. Newitt *Being a Chaplain.* London: SPCK.

Todd, A. (2011) 'Responding to Diversity: Chaplaincy in a Multi-Faith Context.' In M. Threlfall-Holmes and M. Newitt *Being a Chaplain.* London: SPCK.

Todd, A. (2013) 'Preventing the "neutral" chaplain? The potential impact of anti-"extremism" policy on prison chaplaincy.' *Practical Theology, 6* (2), 144–158.

Todd, A., Slater, V. and Dunlop, S. (2014) *The Church of England's Involvement in Chaplaincy: Research Report for The Mission and Public Affairs Council.* Cardiff and Cuddesdon: Cardiff Centre for Chaplaincy Studies and Oxford Centre for Ecclesiology and Practical Theology. Accessed on 7/7/2017 at: http://stmichaels.ac.uk/assets/pdf/Todd__Slater___Dunlop_2014_Report_on_Church_of_England_Chaplaincy.pdf.

5

EMBEDDING CHAPLAINCY
Integrity and Presence
——————— MARGARET WHIPP ———————

Mythologies of mission

The story goes that after nine years of war and a long-drawn out siege, the wily Greeks resorted to subterfuge to gain entrance to the ancient city of Troy. Presented as a thank-offering to Athena, Odysseus' famous Trojan Horse was actually a cunning agent of infiltration, allowing direct access to the impregnable city under cover of darkness for hundreds of highly trained hostile forces. We have learned to be wary of Greeks bearing gifts.

The ostensive 'gift' of chaplaincy touches deep-rooted cultural nerves of suspicion. It would be naive to reckon otherwise. It is against this acutely suspicious contemporary backdrop that I wish to explore the integrity of the 'mission' which is offered. Bishop Alan Wilson compares the churches, expecting an unequivocal welcome for their ministry, to a dodgy plumber, who insists on being paid in cash, believing that clients will accept his stance as a mark of traditional rectitude rather than questionable character (Wilson 2015). The hard reality for many extra-parochial ministers is that the institutions that host chaplains have learned to be profoundly wary of the ulterior motives that bring them within their gates. In many professions, this suspicion of religious agendas is actively taught, while in wider public debate a presumption of self-interest and shady lack of accountability is routinely associated with any personnel and services that come sponsored by a religious organisation.

Chaplaincy as 'mission' is now rarely regarded as good news, and more frequently as potentially dangerous infiltration. In my own context of healthcare, it is evident that the National Secular Society's relentless polemic against religious 'intrusion' has found broad, if unquestioning, acceptance (National Secular Society 2012). Its argument goes that Christian chaplains – provided and paid for by the taxpayer – are at best representatives of religious partiality, providing services only for the favoured elect, and at worst agents of indoctrination, preying unethically on vulnerable patients in pursuit of their own underhand proselytising agenda.

While serious questions of probity hang over all representatives of religious communities, it is not surprising that secularity has become the new benchmark for safety – morally, professionally, and, above all, reputationally and politically – in almost every area of public life. Faced with widespread de-recognition of any automatic right of access, and doubts about transparency that are not entirely unfounded, it is more important than ever for religious sponsors to embrace and articulate a theology of chaplaincy which is genuinely committed to service and acutely sensitive to the imperialistic overtones of missional discourse in our largely, and uncomfortably, post-Christian society.

The reflections in this chapter will be rooted in my particular experience of healthcare chaplaincy and my vocational commitment as a Christian priest within the Church of England. However, as someone who is glad to have led ecumenical and multi-faith teams within higher education as well as hospital chaplaincies, I hope that many points of deeper and broader reflection may emerge for readers whose faith and practice is located and experienced differently. My guiding purpose in this chapter will be to develop a critical theology of chaplaincy, beginning with the provocative image of 'embedded' mission.

Between the sheets of institutional chaplaincy

It was Paul Ballard in 2009 who first promoted the model of chaplaincy as an 'embedded' mode of mission (Ballard 2009). His image, drawn from the media, had first come to prominence during television coverage of the 2003 invasion of Iraq. Disappointed by low levels of access negotiated in the previous Gulf War, US media groups agreed contracts with the military curtailing any disclosures that might compromise the safety of troops, or the success of ongoing strategy, in return for an unprecedented freedom of access for reporters and photographers within the fiercest combat zones. The resulting frontline attachments set a new standard for vivid and incisive battlefield journalism.

The heroic image of the 'embedded' journalist soon became a media success story. But with success came inevitable criticisms of their unthinkingly carnal image. Who, exactly, were these reporters in bed with? And what price was being paid in terms of unbiased objectivity in return for their cosy relationships of military protection and privilege? The debate was about integrity and purity of motive; and for that reason, a very illuminating parallel for ascetic reflection on the mission of chaplaincies which are, all too frequently, besmirched by similar suspicions.

Reputational integrity and personal trust are the *sine quibus non* (indispensable conditions) for every effective chaplain. These virtues, I suggest, will be matters of vocational disposition and character rather more than of ecclesiological structure and theology. The chaplain's chastity of purpose, stability of presence, and poverty of power – the ascetic hallmarks of any genuinely disinterested ministry – embody the same rigorous repudiation of self-interest as the classic monastic missions, calling us beyond the hidden imperialism of the Trojan Horse model of infiltration. Taking ascetical theology, then, as a point of departure, I shall explore the subtle virtues of the embedded chaplain in relation to the character of her presence, her professionalism and her power.

Subtleties of presence

Infiltrating or serving? The metaphor of embeddedness points, at its best, to the values of a faithful presence. To 'embed' something is to fix it firmly or deeply within a surrounding mass (like fossils within a rock), to implant an idea so that it becomes ingrained within a particular context (like an educational objective within a curriculum), or to insert an object as an integral part of a surrounding whole (like a subordinate clause within a sentence, or a microprocessor within a desktop computer).

Presence counts. In one of the more radical twentieth-century experiments in workplace ministry, the *Mission de France* embedded worker-priests amid the sweat and grime of northern industrial docklands. Stripped of all their priestly trappings, their mission was simply to belong: to live and move and have their being among the other heavy manual workers. 'But what did they actually do?' asked the curious English bishop when he interviewed the worker-priests' superior. Abbé Godin's emphatic reply caught the entire spirit of the movement: *'C'est la présence. C'est la présence!'* (Edwards 1961, p.126).

Presence matters. Woody Allen famously quipped that 80 per cent of life consists of showing up (Allen 2008). This is what we cherish as one of the keenest principles of incarnational theology – that presence precedes function. The real human presence of Christ – 'which we have heard, which we have seen with our eyes, which we have looked at and touched with our hands' (1 John 1.1) – reveals the transformative power of God's own being, and dwelling, among us.

The chaplain's presence, however, is scarcely navigated without problems. Paul Ballard rehearses the challenge of steering between the twin perils of an over-identification with management objectives which threaten to blunt our prophetic edge and a ministry on the margins of institutional or industrial life which is too irrelevant to cut any ice. 'This is, of course, precisely the tension of the incarnation – of being in the world so entirely that there is identity, and yet being "not of this world" so as to be free to serve it' (Ballard 2009, p.21). In Niebuhrian terms, chaplains must negotiate a subtle course between the twin poles of cosy assimilation and crude opposition in order to find their true missional integrity (Niebuhr 1951).

The presencing of good news in this way requires a supreme generosity of spirit which, to sustain the incarnational analysis, must be sincerely kenotic, offering a truly disinterested service to the host institution. Elaine Graham, describing the contribution of religious voices in public space as 'between a rock and a hard place', highlights the cogency of an 'apologetics of presence' when it is embodied in public vocations which are transparently 'more interested in the wellbeing of the human family than in winning a [self serving] argument' (2016).

We shall need to explore the nature of this apologetic 'presence' in some depth and detail in order to build a sufficiently robust practical theology for chaplaincy. The time-honoured posture of 'loitering with intent' hints at the possibilities, but is not nearly subtle enough to direct those complex and delicate balances which contemporary chaplains must discern on a day-to-day basis if they are to be faithful to their vocation.

The first, and essential, characteristic of presence is *faithfulness*. The embedded chaplain grows to become, in the best sense of the word, something of a fixture in her organisation. She represents the Benedictine virtue of stability, offering a pastoral point of anchorage in a sea of change. For a patient, in a fast-paced modern hospital, where nurses, doctors and fellow patients come and go at an alarming speed, the reassuring continuity of a relationship with the chaplain can be a deep stabiliser through critical times. A similar sense of personal reassurance and regard is embodied by many school chaplains who see their students through year after year of rapidly changing educational demands. In a world of strangers, the pastor's steady presence of 'being there' brings a precious and faithful personal gift.

This faithful, dependable presence in a particular time and space is an investment not to be entered into lightly. It marks an important distinction from the current vogue for fresh or alternative models of mission which John Caperon describes as 'para-chaplaincy'. This visiting, as opposed to embedded, model is:

> essentially an externally provided chaplaincy, where the chaplain is separate from the institution; the chaplain's understanding of faith is shaped not by the [school's] ethos or its formal ecclesial identity but by the sponsoring church or charity from which he or she is sent. (Caperon 2015)

Para-chaplaincies, which send in their troops to prisons, schools and universities offer a highly targeted form of mission that is set largely on their own terms. They will bring in their own patterns of theology and accountability, setting powerful boundaries of availability and practice, which may or may not be of genuine service to the institution. They seek a fruitful ministry, often cherry-picking opportunities for engagement that will further a particular evangelistic agenda, bringing kudos to their sponsoring organisation. This may be to exaggerate the contrast, but the point is of crucial importance that 'hit and run' styles of mission will be regarded with deep, and entirely reasonable, suspicion by their host communities.

The alternative vision of faithfulness, or stability of presence, is about putting down roots, slowly and deeply, into the terroir of the institution, in all its uniqueness and subtlety. This slow presencing shapes the chaplain's journey towards an authentic level of trust that is only gained through knowledge and respect for the institution's own values and accountability structures, and a pattern of care that reflects her willingness to submit to the institution's rhythms of life and service.

Learning the heartbeat of her institution, and speaking its language like a native, the faithful chaplain comes to embody a very different kind of faithful loving kindness from the entrepreneurial model of visiting evangelists. 'Seeking the good of the city' (Jeremiah 29.7), she commits to a genuine and enduring relationship which I have described elsewhere in terms of being human, being present and being good news (Whipp 2013, p.11ff).

The second characteristic of presence, and one which is very hard to pin down, is the archetypal quality which Steve Nolan has dubbed the chaplain's *evocative presence* (Nolan 2012, p.36ff). In my first week as a hospital chaplain I was warmly greeted by the outpatient sister who explained, 'You're there to remind us.' At that point my new colleague knew almost nothing of my skills or sensitivities, my theological or pastoral capacity; yet my visible presence as a priest within her department prompted a powerful evocation of the moral and spiritual foundations for her own vocation.

This symbolic capacity is something which ministers of religion bear at the heart of their representative calling. Psychologically and spiritually, they stand for God. In theological terms, the hospital chaplain provides what Austin Farrer helpfully described as a 'walking sacrament' (Farrer 1991) evoking deep intuitions of faith and hope, compassion and peace, reconciliation and yearned-for healing in patients and staff alike. The visit of the chaplain, at a deep and archetypal level, represents an immediate and tangible visitation from God.

Of course, the subtleties of such a profoundly transferential relationship will be delicate and difficult to handle with grace. Drawing on the terminology of classic psychoanalysis, Nolan elucidates a complex blend of positive and negative projections which may play upon the figure of the chaplain at the bedside – from an intense flood of emotional relief, to studied indifference, or unrestrained rage. The spiritual work of the chaplain is to receive or, better, to embrace such projections with compassion and faithfulness. In Nolan's research he identifies a twin task, which reflects the tensions of an incarnational role in both 'staying with' the intensity of positive or negative projections, while also remaining authentically grounded in the particular human truth of 'being me' (Nolan 2012, p.54).

This kind of spiritual work and symbolic representation will be subtly different from the comparable psychotherapeutic task of working with transference and countertransference, where the frame of reference is purely humanistic. The religious chaplain who bears with, and wrestles with, but also prays with the projections of those in her care – often at times of the most acute human vulnerability and awe – does so with all the priestliness of someone who personally relates to the living God whom she represents. Far from being a blank canvas on which the religious phantasies of her client may – more or less helpfully – play out, the priest's commitment to evocative presence requires her to draw deeply on the resources of faith, and hope, and love which can feed their hunger for authentic communion. This can be costly, and often courageous, spiritual work.

The third subtle characteristic of the chaplain's presence is a necessary liminality. Being willing to linger somewhat on the edge of things, while striving to be genuinely embedded in context, is a paradoxical path for the chaplain to patrol. Hers will not be a role which can be neatly defined or pigeonholed. In the hospital, for example, she must tread the margins of clinically organised time and space, navigating those interstitial byways where the subtleties of the spirit may be discerned and encouraged. Any hubristic rush to clarify her contribution in terms of professional protocols will usually be counterproductive. She is not there to buttress her own position. Instead, she stands poised on the raw edges of human crisis and questioning, a ready guide for the searching human soul.

This marks a noticeably different stance from that of the parish priest, so often the focal centre of action within his own building and schedule of meetings. Even in statutory chaplaincies, blessed and burdened with all the authority of history and establishment, the role of the chaplain remains fraught with ambiguities as she upholds some measure of necessary detachment from those authority dynamics which could compromise her usefulness.

The boundaries of this subtle liminality can be especially confusing where the outworkings of institutional power – in schools and prisons, for example – can be all-pervading. So there remains a vitally ascetic discipline in the chaplain's determination not to be co-opted to every agenda of the institutional structures within which she serves. Managerially, for that reason, chaplaincy is often a muddle. And ecclesiologically, it will be an inevitable mess. But pastorally, the chaplain who learns to be at ease with her liminality will be privileged to witness the profound intermingling of faith and frailty on some of the most awesome boundaries of life and death itself.

The fourth aspect of presence which the chaplain embodies is an exquisite attentiveness. She is not an idle, or apathetic presence in the institution, but someone constantly alert to its spiritual wellbeing. The chaplain must be present in order to watch and wait, attending to the full business of human life – with a quiet hope of nurturing life in all its fullness. But her curiosity must be carefully restrained: any intrusiveness, physical or spiritual, will destroy the delicate trust which is essential for her craft. Her discipline is to watch ceaselessly, like the birdwatcher in his hide, without startling or disrupting those whose ongoing life and work she is there to bless.

Once again, the sheer subtleties of this prayerful presence exemplify the unique charism of chaplaincy. One of the most useful mantras I ever learned was that 'chaplains walk slowly'. Being attentive requires a quality of calm and stillness, even countercultural leisure, which the chaplain preserves amid the frenetic busyness of hard-working communities. Taking the time to listen, and to attend deeply, will hone her keenest skills of spiritual discernment and authentic compassion. This ceaseless attention is where the hard work of seeking out new relationships – in the hospital context, for example, through the steady encouragement of patient referrals – blends with the softer skills of pastoral conversation which will guide those relationships towards a surprising level of spiritual depth.

Infiltrating or serving? The character of embodied and embedded presence which the chaplain brings to her host community raises profound and subtle questions of pastoral integrity. I am advocating in this chapter a depth of moral and spiritual generosity which reflects the kenotic quality of the incarnation in a model of chaplaincy which is faithful, evocative, liminal and attentive. Building on these personal virtues of presence, I shall now explore the related question of the chaplain's competence and professionalism.

A subtle professionalism

The shifting meanings encompassed by the word 'professional' offer a helpful way in to the current and contentious debate about the 'professionalisation' of chaplaincy. This is a word that, etymologically, reflects first and foremost a declaration of belief or, still more seriously, the declaration or vows made on entry to a religious order, and has evolved over time towards a designation for occupational groups characterised by intensive training and exclusive qualification. When we speak of a professional calibre, or of professional competence and skill, we are indicating a degree of knowledge and a standard of behaviour that reflects a strenuous level of occupational expertise and accountability.

Professions are powerful groups. Having studied, qualified, and practised for many years as a medical consultant, I entertain no doubts concerning the weight of personal and political power that is invested in the various professional groups within my own sphere of healthcare. Nor can I be naive about the perennial temptations to competition and self-advancement which beset professional healthcare workers who must be concerned to maximise and maintain the power of their roles. These are basic sociological realities.

What, then, are we to make of the aim to 'professionalise' chaplaincy? The application in 2016 by the UK Board of Healthcare Chaplaincy for Voluntary Professional Registration with the Professional Standards Authority (UKBHC 2016) represents the latest move in a long history of increasingly self-conscious professionalisation within this particular sector (see Swift 2014, pp.29–51). Amid the highly differentiated and multidisciplinary world of professional healthcare there is a strong pressure to define and delineate a specific bandwidth of professional expertise which can properly be upheld as the business of chaplains. Pursuing my inquiry into ascetical theology as an important guide for the chaplain's disposition and character, I turn now to cast a critical eye over these aspirations. Is the mantle of professionalism the best guarantor of disinterested service, or is it another cloak for the questionable infiltration of a Trojan Horse?

There can be nothing wrong with the drive towards professionalisation, which provides a healthy corrective to the worst kinds of bumbling amateurism. We have seen too many well-intentioned but poorly informed and lamentably ill-disciplined, paid as well as voluntary, religious personnel who make a poor showing as chaplains. What concerns me at this point, though, are the anxiously professional chaplains who protest too much, rushing uncritically to resolve the paradox of liminality by joining the 'me too' club of self-promoting disciplinary experts. When the embedded chaplain strives too hard to adopt the mantle of a professional among professionals, she will face serious and subtle temptations to her distinctively ascetic integrity.

The first and most obvious temptation is that of *elitism*. George Bernard Shaw was writing about doctors when he made his famous indictment that 'all professions are conspiracies against the laity' (Shaw 1911, p.106). Just as physicians require patients to be sick in order to build up their prestige and power, so those who practise the cure of souls can develop an unhealthy paternalism towards those who seek their care. There is a not-so-thinly veiled arrogance in much of the contemporary discourse of spiritual care. The extension of a medical model in order to delineate so-called 'spiritual needs' or, more potently, to seek to 'diagnose' and 'intervene' in spiritual distress suggests a worryingly condescending attitude towards our neighbours who, in times of crisis, are taking their share in the common realities of this raw and troubling human existence. Who am I, as a would-be professional in these matters, to presume to 'make them better'?

Bearing a common humanity means there is a subtle balance to strike for any chaplain who seeks, on the one hand, to develop a depth of personal and spiritual wisdom in order to attend generously to those in her care, while on the other hand retaining a sincere humility in the face of those unique mysteries of human life and death which it is her privilege to witness. In the face of dreadful suffering, for example, no honest chaplain can pretend to be anything other than a poor amateur – trusting that in the original sense of that misrepresented term (the word meant *a lover* long before it acquired the connotations of someone unskilled in their task) it will be the caring *amateur* who most genuinely represents the warm heart and personal investment of compassion. Any hint of professional superiority will perversely undermine the deep solidarity in human vulnerability that is the chaplain's most priceless gift.

The second temptation inherent within many professional perspectives is that of *reductionism*. Professionals, like rulers of state, develop power and influence by staking out clear borders within which to reign supreme. It is in their interests to define a territory within which their knowledge base, and their particular craft, can hold sway. Surgeons look for operations that they have the tools to perform, just as surely as social workers look out for housing difficulties that they have the skills to resolve. There is a subtle temptation for chaplains to collude with the agenda that wants to ring-fence 'spirituality' as a manageable specialty among other specialties.

In our hypermodern society of intense differentiation of professional know-how, the extent of ultra-specialisation is not always benign. We are all familiar with the caricature of the doctor who knows all there is to know about the fifth toe on the left foot but is clueless about any other aspect of human biology. The problems of fragmentation are especially disturbing when human beings face a burden of personal suffering or existential crisis which is so weighty and all-pervading that it will overwhelm any one professional's capacity to resolve.

Tidy-minded chaplains may secretly long for the kind of role definition that could circumscribe their field of expertise within readily described boundaries. Knowing and articulating what you are good at can be immensely empowering. It is not surprising, therefore, (and not necessarily wrong) that chaplains should seek to bolster the inherent insecurity of their vocational position by training in some specific therapeutic technique – whether it be mental health advocacy or mindfulness. The temptation to present as a skilled technician among other skilled technicians can be all but impossible to resist.

There is something of unspeakable value, however, in the chaplain's determination to maintain a holistic human vision, caring for the whole person with the whole person. In particular, the chaplain must resist the compartmentalised way of thinking that tries to carve off a set of narrowly defined objectives as the specific target area for her 'spiritual care'. This type of reductionism is a peculiarly modern heresy which has taken root in many areas of healthcare, as professional managers strive to corral and control the transcendent vitality and sheer messiness of authentic relationships of pastoral care (Nolan 2009).

The third temptation, closely related to a philosophical reductionism, is an occupational bias towards *functionalism* – presenting chaplains as technicians of the spirit, rather than as bearers of an office within the community. One of the obvious drivers towards this kind of shallow functionalism is activity monitoring – whether undertaken for the sake of performance management or for the related purpose of 'evidence-based' contributions to research.

It is important to expose the underlying value bias whenever benchmarks of activity are defined and measured. Put simply, we know that it is far easier to demonstrate a level of business in terms of quantitatively objective functional measures, such as the number of ward visits undertaken by an individual chaplain, rather than in the more searching terms of the depth of spiritual value represented by a profound quality of accompanying presence. The latter is much harder to articulate and commend, but arguably of far greater importance for the distinctive service offered by the chaplain.

I have in my sights here some of the cruder articulations of 'outcome-oriented chaplaincy' which perversely reduce rather than expand our vision for human life in all its fullness (see Van de Creek and Lucas 2012). There is a pressing temptation, within a scientifically and bureaucratically driven and resourced environment, to reduce the practices of spiritual care to some Procrustean bed of objectively measurable 'interventions' and reliably achievable 'outcomes'. This is fundamentally wrong-headed, an iron cage that constrains the glorious freedom of the individual soul and the unpredictably rich journey of spiritual maturity that requires a deeper listening and a larger language than any catalogue of interventions and associated outcomes can neatly circumscribe.

A subtle purpose

Underlying my argument in this chapter is a distinctively theological vision of the purpose of embedded chaplaincy, which informs the ascetic lens through which I have been raising questions of integrity and practice.

In closing I return to the underpinning model of mission, firmly rejecting any of the underhand motivations represented by the Trojan Horse mentality, in favour of a genuinely disinterested and kenotic model of open-hearted *hospitality*. In the widest sense possible, with the most subtle arts at her disposal, the chaplain's purpose is to make room for the spirit (cf. Pohl 1999).

We have some venerable historical precedents to inform what this might look like in our modern institutional context where the chaplain is positioned, paradoxically, as both host and guest. I am recalling the ancient hospitallers who made room for pilgrims, providing warmth and protection on a perilous journey, along with subtle ambassadorial support and spiritual sustenance. And I am thinking, of course, of the visionary legacy of the modern hospice movement, with its bold and compassionate reimagining of the practical and spiritual needs and opportunities of pilgrims on their journey towards death.

In public services the subtle work of hospitality must be radically, and genuinely, dialogical. There will be no room for exclusive labels of religious identity or reductive designations of spiritual distress. The only valid stance for an embedded chaplain is to welcome, in a totally disinterested way, any and every authentically human encounter – simply and sincerely for what it is.

This model of the hospitable chaplain, who offers herself first and foremost as being human, being present and being good news, presents a uniquely personal challenge and privilege. Neither purposeless nor protocol-bound, the chaplain embraces each day with the spiritual freedom and expectancy that anticipates the presence of Christ in the encounter. For a suggestive image, I draw on Miroslav Volf's beautifully subtle drama of embrace (Volf 1996, pp.140–145).

An embrace begins with a gesture of welcome. The one offering her greeting stands with open arms, making space emotionally and spiritually for another person to engage. Next follows a period of waiting. Will the offer be taken up? Or will the other person turn away? The chaplain is always vulnerable to disinterest or disdain. But if she finds a reciprocating engagement, then some kind of open-heartedness, some human tenderness can be exchanged. Two people become fully present, each to the other. A moment of intimacy, akin to the softness of embrace, allows them to share in an expression of deeper joys and struggles and cares. This moment must not be greedily prolonged, however. It is a time for understanding and communion, but not an occasion for possession and control. The embrace ends, therefore, as intentionally as it began, with the opening up and active release of letting go. What transpires in the depths of embrace is not hers to prescribe or evaluate. It can only be a blessing of grace.

This is the disposition and presence of a generous chaplain who is embedded for the service of individuals, of her institution, and of a divine Spirit. She is not a Trojan Horse: still less an empire builder. She is an ascetic witness to the vision and the practice of life in all its fullness, through the generous and subtle hospitality of her own presence, her professionalism and her purposeful and profoundly human encounters.

References

Allen, W. (2008) *Vicky Christina Barcelona* Interview. S. Weintraub. Accessed on 7/7/2017 at: http://collider.com/woody-allen-interview-vicky-cristina-barcelona.

Ballard, P. (2009) 'Locating chaplaincy: a theological note.' *Crucible* July–September 2009: 18–24.

Caperon, J. (2015) 'Education Chaplaincy: Case Study.' In C. Swift, M. Cobb and A. Todd *A Handbook of Chaplaincy Studies*. Aldershot and Burlington, VT: Ashgate.

Edwards, D.L. (ed.) (1961) *Priests and Workers: An Anglo-French Discussion.* London: SCM Press.

Farrer, A. (1991) 'Walking Sacraments.' In L. Holden (ed.) *Austin Farrer: The Essential Sermons.* London: SPCK.

Graham, E. (2016) 'Between a Rock and a Hard Place: Negotiating Religious Voices in Public Places.' Address to Modern Church Council, 2016. Availabe at: http://modernchurch.org.uk.

National Secular Society (2012) *Costing the Heavens.* Available at: www.secularism.org.uk/uploads/nhs-chaplaincy-funding.html.

Niebuhr, H.R. (1951) *Christ and Culture.* New York: Harper & Row.

Nolan, S. (2009) 'In defence of the indefensible: an alternative to John Paley's reductionist, atheistic, psychological alternative to spirituality.' *Nursing Philosophy 10* (3): 203–13.

Nolan, S. (2012) *Spiritual Care at the End of Life: The Chaplain as a 'Hopeful Presence'.* London: Jessica Kingsley Publishers.

Pohl, C. (1999) *Making Room: Recovering Hospitality as a Christian Tradition.* Grand Rapids: Eerdmans.

Shaw, G.B. (1911) *The Doctor's Dilemma.* London: Constable.

Swift, C. (2014) *Hospital Chaplaincy in the Twenty-First Century.* Aldershot: Ashgate.

UK Board of Healthcare Chaplaincy (2016) 'Application for Voluntary Professional Registration.' Accessed on 7/7/2017 at: www.ukbhc.org.uk/chaplains.

Van de Creek, L. and Lucas, A.M. (2012) *The Discipline for Pastoral Care Giving: Foundations for Outcome Oriented Chaplaincy.* New York: Routledge.

Volf, M. (1996) *Exclusion and Embrace: Theological Exploration of Identity, Otherness and Reconciliation.* Nashville: Abingdon.

Whipp, M. (2013) *SCM Studyguide: Pastoral Theology.* London: SCM Press.

Wilson, A. (2015) Churches and plumbers. Private communication.

6

CHAPLAINCY AND TRADITIONAL CHURCH STRUCTURES

JOHN CAPERON

So far this book has offered a range of theological perspectives on chaplaincy. It has been argued that the incarnation itself prompts us to recognise the Christological character of humanity, and that chaplaincy both fully shares and expresses the four marks of the Church as One, Holy, Catholic and Apostolic. Chaplaincy stands at the forefront of multi-faith engagement in the present age, it has also been argued, prompting a 'generous orthodoxy' of Christian belief. Considering the range of possible theological and secular models of chaplaincy, it has been suggested that chaplaincy ministers in a particular way to 'humanity's innate need for relationships'. And in exploring the nature of 'embedded' chaplaincy, it has been argued that the chaplain's 'prayerful presence' is 'an ascetic witness to the vision and the practice of life in all its fullness'. In short, chaplaincy's specific identity is of huge significance for the Church's ministry and mission in the twenty-first century.

But the fact remains that chaplaincy is still often regarded as something of a sideshow to the established Church's central, traditional understanding of ministry as being rooted in parish and church, vicar and people. At a time when chaplaincy is rapidly developing as both a lay and a clerical ministry, incorporating both secular and multi-faith elements (Ryan 2015), the question then inevitably arises: how much can the Church's traditional structures still offer? As a worker-priest, I have been extensively involved in parish life and ministry, in addition to experiencing chaplaincy in my own professional context of secondary education (Caperon 2015). From this dual perspective, I aim in this chapter to explore what the institutional Church needs to treasure from its parochial inheritance, and what it must learn from chaplaincy if its understanding of ministry is to be appropriate to the present age. My focus is explicitly on chaplaincy as a genre of ordained Christian ministry.

Parish and vicar: resonant traditional institutions

The parish system is indelibly imprinted on the English landscape. The church towers and spires visible from motorways and railway lines speak of a whole pattern of inherited tradition whose influence has shaped our communities and culture. However far the much-debated process of secularisation may now have reached, it remains hard to imagine 'England' and English culture without the parish church and the vicar.

The role of 'vicar' still resonates in English popular culture. And while this may be particularly true in rural settings, the common assumption still seems to be that 'the vicar' is a person (a 'parson') who has a recognised, respected place within the local community. He or she is someone whose religious and spiritual role retains validity, who is evidently committed to the welfare of others and to the support of community life, as well as to the institution of the Church. Even nationally reported clerical sexual abuse seems not to have damaged general perceptions of the role, just that of aberrant, individual officeholders. Recent media presentations of the vicar's role have been overwhelmingly favourable. Dawn French's rural

Vicar of Dibley is affectionately portrayed; Tom Hollander's down-to-earth Rev wavers in faith but is strongly committed to pastoral ministry in his East London parish; and the vicar-sleuth hero of ITV's *Grantchester* reveals real spiritual struggle as a key element in his encounters with crime.

The idea of 'parish' still resonates, too: a knowable community, a place of neighbours and friends of 'all sorts and conditions'. While this may carry an element of nostalgia for a vanished rural past, a sense of parish as the basis of community is locked into our political system, with parish councils being the base level of (rural) local government. Nor is it that long since 'the parish' carried significant responsibilities within the social order, as an agency of social support, and as the context for licensing adult unions. The phrases 'on the parish' and 'of this parish' still have some currency, and whenever banns for a forthcoming wedding are called in a parish church the rooted structures of the past are implicitly invoked.

Institutions and significance

But what exactly do parish and vicar embody? A continuing affectionate, even cosy regard for 'the vicar' may not be the only resonance, for there are ambiguities in these traditional institutions from which, it is arguable, chaplaincy may be free. The pastoral-administrative terms 'diocese' and 'parish' are traceable back to the administration of the later Roman Empire, when the Church, freed from persecution, quite naturally adopted imperial terminology and structures. Similarly, the roles of bishop and priest were in part shaped by imperial magistracy (MacCulloch 2009, pp.196–97). So, deep in the institutions of parish and vicar there lie suggestions not just of pastoral care and oversight, but also of rule and governance.

The 'cure of souls' traditionally shared by the bishop with his 'curates' or parish priests may sound as if pastoral care or 'cure' is the core significance of being a vicar, but hints of power and rule are never far away: the Church of England still employs the term 'interregnum' when one vicar has left and another is to be inducted. At one level, vicars offer care, but at another, they rule. These hints of power carried real force until quite recently; the nineteenth-century clerical magistrate was a common feature of the civil order, handing out legal punishment to local malefactors. Though the current Ordinal describes the calling of priests as being 'servants and shepherds among the people to whom they are sent', common usage refers to a vicar 'running a parish', suggesting the exercise of managerial – if not magisterial – authority.

And somewhere in the notion of the parish lies the idea of a place not just of known relationships and community, but also of a limited and limiting locality. There may be regular reported instances of village communities coming together to resist change, with protest meetings held in the parish church against proposed new housing developments or mineral exploitation: the parish can still be an active community. But the common use of the word 'parochial', meaning 'of limited vision', 'domestic', even 'petty', tells a story: in reality, a parish may be a place of enclosed and limited opportunity. If once the parish was the place of security, its bounds regularly beaten to demonstrate the extent of the known community, those boundaries are now largely invisible and disregarded, except by the Church, for whom they still mark the limits of a vicar's authority. So the idea of parish as a mixed community bound together by place, residence and common interest is more nostalgic ideal than current reality. It scarcely needs adding that freedom from the authority role of vicar and from the limitations of parish may for some be a real attraction to the ministerial sphere of chaplaincy.

Church and community

The Church of England still draws on this nostalgic ideal in its website strapline: 'A Christian presence in every community.' The Church's care, this suggests, still covers the whole nation, despite what national church attendance statistics may suggest. There is a church in every parish, and wherever you are in England, you are within the sphere of the Church's ministry. The Church of England, it seems to say, is for everyone, everywhere; it is a national, territorial church and embraces all within its parishes who will accept its ministry. This ongoing territorial commitment is evident; but the website avoids the word 'parish' – aware perhaps of the negative implications of the term – and the use of 'community' instead is interesting.

'Community' has a complex and shifting meaning. It can carry the general sense of 'society'; and more specifically 'a body of people organised into a particular group'. It has also conveyed the idea of shared living and common ownership, as in a religious community; and by the late nineteenth century it had been extended to cover the idea of a specific religious or racial group, as in 'the Jewish community'. Ideas of locality, common identity and shared interest are all included in current usage: 'community' conveys a positive sense of involvement and identity, as in 'the local community'; and usage such as 'the LGBTI (lesbian, gay, bisexual, trans and intersex) community' both identifies a specific interest group and also helps convey a sense of belonging for its members. 'Community' can therefore suggest not only locality, but also associational identity.

So although the obvious intended meaning of the Church of England's website strapline refers to *local* community, it carries a wider implication. For 'community' is not just about locality – it is also about association, identity, membership and group belonging. It seems clear that the Church of England wants to identify itself publicly as a church of locality, of territory. But the reality is that the 'communities' of England are both local and associational; formed both by locality and by all the other social factors – shared interests and activities – that bring people together. But does the Church's self-understanding sufficiently incorporate a vision encompassing not just geographical locality but also the whole of society in all its diverse associations and networks?

Debating the Church's mission and ministry

How the Church understands and envisions its mission and ministry is a core question, and one that has been vigorously debated since the beginning of this century. Traditional assumptions about parish and vicar were first challenged in *Mission-Shaped Church* (Cray 2004). Identifying the changing context of the 'networked' twenty-first century and the 'postmodern era' as major challenges to the Church of England's traditional pattern of a parish ministry rooted in place, this report argued that a truly 'mission-shaped church' would look to 'fresh expressions' of church, to 'new ways of being church' in the networks and communities of society, to 'church plants' rather than to traditional parish structures. Seeing the static, territorial model of church as outdated, *Mission-Shaped Church* in effect proposed its replacement by a dynamic model in which new churches and church plants would be centres of evangelism and growth. To one critic, however, this was more about 'church-shaped mission' than 'mission-shaped church' (Hull 2006), the emphasis being still on 'churches' rather than on the wider society which the Church is called to serve.

The Future of the Parish System (Croft 2006) offered a conservative and stabilising response to the challenge of *Mission-Shaped Church*. One key contributor to the volume, the then archbishop of Canterbury Rowan Williams, presented a positive picture of what the traditional parish model of ministry could still provide. He envisaged 'a group of worshippers within every 'natural' community in a country, trying to let that community know what kind of God it worships and what, as a result, is possible for human beings' (Williams 2006, p.53). Affirming this outward-looking vision rooted in the traditional pattern, Williams suggested that 'parochial presence' was the embodiment of its vocation of service to the whole community.

The idea that parochial ministry represented the Church's time-honoured commitment to society, expressed in the continuing presence of the parish church and vicar, was further explored by Martyn Percy. Arguing that 'it would be premature to sound the death-knell for the parish church', he pointed to the importance of 'maintaining religion as something that is public, accessible and extensive, while also being distinct, intensive and mysterious'. Percy argued that '... in the complex, porous and ambiguous spaces of our future, the Church will need to find its places in society once again, if it is to continue to offer a religion that is public, performative and pastoral'. The central issue was 'ensuring that ministries engage with people' (Percy 2006, pp.12–15), and the prime locus of this engagement would remain the parish, the locality. What is fascinating about both these contributions is that without mentioning chaplaincy, they drew on two concepts central to its theology: presence and engagement.

The most outspoken reassertion of the parish model of mission and ministry, presented as a riposte to 'fresh expressions' thinking, was *For the Parish* (Davison and Milbank 2010). Identifying what they saw as theological, ecclesiological and sociological shortcomings in *Mission-Shaped Church*, Davison and Milbank highlighted the importance of the 'practices and disciplines of the inherited church', defending the concept of the parish as a mixed, varied and socially comprehensive community and contrasting it with the 'special interest groups' which, they argued, 'fresh expressions of church' essentially were (Davison and Milbank 2010, p.vii). Their vigorously argued book dismissed *Mission-Shaped Church* as both superficial and over-reliant on an evangelical theological perspective that failed to acknowledge the significance of Catholic tradition in the ongoing continuity of the 'inherited' Church.

What the different participants in this debate generally failed to acknowledge, though, was that varying models of church and ministry might reflect different social contexts. The most traditional of these – the rural village – was perhaps inevitably the one where a traditional pattern of ministry might seem most in place. Here, particularly in villages fortunate enough still to be places of work as well as retirement, locations for genuine social class interaction rather than being socially and economically monochrome, the church might still be the locus for community worship and the vicar still a friend to all – the Dibley world. In the urban, inner-city context, with the vicar being possibly the only professional person in a downtown, deprived parish – the world of 'Rev' – things were different. And they were different again in the prosperous suburbs, where 'successful' and growing churches, often evangelical and/or charismatic, were able to assemble an eclectic membership, drawn together by the vigorous social identity of 'church' and a strong sense of a shared gospel to be spread to others.

But what was most remarkable about the debate around ministry and mission was that it singularly failed to consider the place of chaplaincy as a genre of ministry, one which is both inevitably responsive to context and also rooted in pastoral presence. Key contributors had highlighted the need for the Church's ministry to be engaged with society, but none seemed to recognise that chaplaincy provided a paradigm in which engagement with the varying associational contexts of the social world was its very *raison d'être*. Chaplaincy and its distinctive ministry were the absent factors in the debate, which almost reduced to a battle between old and new, tradition and change, between proponents of a Catholic view of the continuing Church, and an energetic, evangelical impulse towards radical change.

The Church's developing agenda on ministry and mission

The debate about ministry and mission emerged at the end of the first decade of the century as a key policy issue for the Church of England's General Synod. In a context of still declining attendance figures and reduced numbers of ordinands, *Challenges for the New Quinquennium* (House of Bishops 2011), took a serious look at the nature of the Church's ministry and mission, concluding with a firm recommitment to the traditional, territorial view. 'The Church of England's vocation is to provide a worshipping and serving Christian presence in every community in the country', it stated. What was emphasised, despite a wider awareness of the networked, associational nature of the new century's society, was community as *locality*: 'the Church's vocation of being present in every part of the land', 'its rootedness at local level'.

Behind this renewed focus on the traditional structures of parochial ministry lay three principles outlined by Archbishop Rowan Williams in his Presidential address to the General Synod in November 2010:

- To take forward the spiritual and numerical growth of the Church of England – including the growth of its capacity to serve the whole community of this country.

- To reshape or reimagine the Church's ministry for the century coming, so as to make sure that there is a growing and sustainable Christian witness in every local community.

- To focus our resources where there is both greatest need and greatest opportunity.

However, these importantly prioritised principles have since then undergone significant modification as they have morphed into official Church policy. Originally, the Williams principles of 2010 balanced a continuing commitment to providing ministry – service – to the 'whole community of this country' with a commitment to seek spiritual and numerical growth in the Church itself. First re-emerging as 'quinquennial goals', then evolving further under the 'Renewal and Reform' (earlier, 'Reform and Renewal') programme inaugurated by the archbishops in 2015, the order and wording have further changed, bringing a greater emphasis on 'mission and the growth of the church', and a prioritisation of 'numerical' over 'spiritual' growth (see Spencer 2015).

Reconceiving ministry and mission

This significant shift of emphasis has meant a profound change in the Church's public agenda, almost a total reconceiving of the concepts of ministry and mission. Instead of an emphasis on serving the whole community in each locality, 'Renewal and Reform' (Church of England 2016) now advocates talk of the Church having a 'missionary agenda'; of the 'need to do mission very urgently'; of the key task for the Church being 'the re-evangelisation of England'; of the priority to 're-structure in order to evangelise the country'. It is as if 'mission' has been reconceived as the narrower concept 'evangelisation'; as if 'ministry' is being understood as 'making disciples'; the service of 'the whole community of the country' being seen as secondary to a focus on boosting the numbers of the gathered church community. Prompted by the demographic decline of the Church of England nationally, it has been argued, numerical growth to ensure survival may now be the national Church's main motivational impulse (Percy 2016).

This has involved a subtle but profound shift in the meaning of the term 'church'. Whereas traditionally 'local church' would have meant 'local church building', it seems now rather to designate the identifiable 'church community' – those who regularly meet for worship in the church building. This indicates a shift from the Church of England's traditional 'societal' ecclesiological model, where all those living in the parish are assumed to be stakeholders in the parish church, to a denominational model in which 'membership' is ascribed to those who actually opt in by attending and contributing to the costs of the church and the parish ministry. This shift from a parochial model to one of the 'gathered congregation' implies that the church community's prime function is to draw others into membership through evangelistic outreach. Thus the local church grows numerically, also thereby increasing financial giving to the Church and providing the resource to maintain the Church's diocesan and managerial structures.

This shift in perspective also involves a marked change in the understanding of what 'ministry' itself consists of. In the societal view, a minister's task is to serve the whole community, seeking out and supporting those in any kind of need within the parish. And if there is still, as I suggested earlier, a degree of affectionate recognition of the role of vicar, this is probably largely to do with the way in which in popular memory that role has been exercised. In the denominational view, however, a minister is reconceived as leader and manager of the church community. No longer is his or her prime concern with the people of the whole parish, but rather with the people in 'his' or 'her' church. For them, he is the source of teaching and advice, the one who 'disciples' them, and whose task is to lead the strategy and resourcing of the gathered church congregation in its mission and evangelisation, designed to bring 'outsiders' in to the church community.

To summarise: we are currently seeing a significant reimagining of mission and ministry, with mission becoming first of all about numerical growth and ministry becoming first of all about evangelisation. Alongside this, there has been a focus on recruiting more professional ministers to enable the Church to continue its traditional commitment to the parish and vicar, to 'a Christian presence in every community'. What has changed, though, is the assumed role of the minister: once the servant of the whole community, she or he is now conceived as the leader of a minority church group within that community.

Ministry and mission in missiological understanding

All this suggests an insufficient engagement by the Church with the theology of mission. Contemporary missiological thinking emphasises that mission is the mission of God, the *missio Dei*, rather than the perceived 'mission' or project of any one church. And this divine mission is about far more than just increasing the numbers of those who attend church. Instead it has to be understood as a divine movement impelling the world towards the Kingdom of God, with the Church being called to collaborate in that mission. This missiological outlook leads to an understanding of the grace of God as already present and active in the world, rather than introduced solely through the Church's activity: in the words of the Second Vatican Council's *Lumen gentium*: '[God] has generously poured out his divine goodness and does not cease to do so' (Abbott 1966, p.585). An Anglican version of this understanding is offered by Paul Avis, who declares that: '*Missio Dei* speaks of the overflowing of the love of God's being and nature into God's purposeful activity in the world' (Avis 2005, p.5). The prevenient reality of *missio Dei* means that '...Christians are not in the futile business of attempting to bring an absent Christ to an abandoned world. God is already ahead of us in mission' (Avis 2005, p.7).

This underlying theological stance points to the real task of the Church being to discern where God is at work in the world, 'already ahead of us in mission'; to celebrate and in the name of Christ to support and continue that work; and through its life of worship and service to bring to the world the good news of God's love and coming Kingdom. There is thus a 'missiological identity' between Christ and the

Church (Avis 2005, p.8), the Church replicating the mission and ministry of Christ in the power of the Holy Spirit. This theology of mission cannot easily accommodate a view of the Church which sees it as the sole dispenser of grace, the company into which people are drawn by evangelistic activity as a place of redemptive safety from the world.

So, the current Church of England emphasis on evangelisation and church growth in the Renewal and Reform programme indicates that the Church has taken a view on mission which is substantially thinner than that of mainstream missiology. Focusing on a single aspect of the Church's calling – the call to evangelisation rooted in the Great Commission of Matthew 28.18–20 – it has chosen to give lower priority to broader concepts of ministry as contributing to human flourishing, to 'life in all its fullness'. This classic Anglican stance sees ministry in terms of pastoral care and service to the world; and in this tradition, the mission of the Church is 'executed through the ministry of word, sacrament and pastoral care' (Avis 2003, p.200). Ministry is to be modelled on the example of the Jesus of the Gospels, the teacher and healer, the Incarnate Son. In contrast, evangelistically focused approaches have arguably drawn the inspiration for their understanding of mission from the Acts of the Apostles and the Letters of St Paul. As so often in theological debate, this is a hermeneutical issue about which parts of the Scriptures are given greatest emphasis.

It is as if the Church of England has been panicked into adopting a missionary agenda by grim church attendance figures and wider attitudinal research portending terminal institutional decline. It is clear that the Church has less claimed adherence in England than in the past two centuries, that adherence is reducing by generation, and that the rate of actual parish church attendance is tiny by comparison with the peak figures of the 1950s. Further, the numbers of those claiming 'no religion' are rising alarmingly. But the simple secularisation thesis – that society becomes less religious all the time – looks less and less convincing in the light of the vibrancy of black Pentecostal churches and the burgeoning social and religious significance of Islam among immigrant communities, not to mention the existence of implicit or vicarious religion (see Bailey 1998). Evidence for the persistence of at least some varieties of religion is strong.

In all these circumstances, it is perfectly possible to understand why the Church is urgently looking to church growth as a key priority. What has been neglected, however, is a more reflective consideration in the light of core missiological understanding of what mission and ministry actually are, and what the Church's vocation actually is. Similarly missing is any substantial consideration of the potential of the specific genre of ministry that is chaplaincy. But chaplaincy's inherent engagement with the structures of society, its location within the varying associational communities of the land, offers a paradigm for ministry and mission that is arguably far richer than the reduced, narrow vision of 'church growth'.

Chaplaincy as a historic form of ministry

What in fact has been quite extraordinary throughout the recent Anglican debate about mission and ministry is the complete absence of any serious consideration of the place of chaplaincy in the Church's ministry in the twenty-first century. Despite the long history of chaplaincy as a specific genre of ministry alongside but distinct from the parochial ministry of the Church, it has had scarcely a mention. But the long and distinctive history of chaplaincy is plain. Karl Rahner, reflecting on the 'passing of the local community' in *Mission and Grace* (Rahner 1963), argues against the widespread assumption – one at the core of the Church of England's current self-understanding – that the Church's activity has always been rooted in territoriality:

...the Church's mission has never simply moved between the local community and the local parish as its beginning and its end...besides the territorial basis there have always been other sociological facts forming the natural foundation for Christian communities. (Rahner 1963, p.58)

Rahner's realisation is that 'other sociological facts' are, and always have been, as significant as locality. And in the present century the parish, once the locus of birth, life and death, no longer shapes our whole existence. Instead, we experience a myriad of associational connections for all kinds of purposes: for work, health, leisure, wellbeing and so on. And while chaplaincy may have originated in locality – in the care of chapels built to preserve relics of St Martin (MacCulloch 2009, p.313) – as a distinctive genre of ministry, it has, since its origins, been in a state of continuing and socially permeating development. Providing ministerial pastoral care and spiritual support within the varying networks and 'natural communities' of society, chaplaincy has embedded itself in changing and varying social contexts, offering a specific kind of ministry: 'ministry where people are' (Westcott House 2013).

The distinctive nature of chaplaincy

But chaplaincy's 'ministry where people are' has been theologically under-explored and under-resourced, with only a handful of theologians offering illuminating insights into chaplaincy's distinctive nature as a genre of ministry. The practical theologian Paul Ballard is one (see also Chapter 5). Ballard notes the 'dispersed' nature of contemporary life, in which 'we move from one sphere to another', and he importantly sees chaplaincy – located in many associational contexts – not as 'an aberration of ministry but an attempt to express the relevance of the gospel to every facet of life'. The chaplaincy model of ministry, he argues, 'is characterised precisely by entering into and working with social structures'

(Ballard 2009, pp.19–20). There is even a case for saying that contemporary chaplaincy echoes in some key respects the early intentions and practices of the parochial system. A vicar represented the Church's ministry and care throughout the locality where people lived, worked and died, interpenetrating its varied social strands and networks. Today, says Ballard, chaplaincy's context is precisely within the varied structures and dispersed communities of the world; whereas the parish priest, situated within the limitations of the local community, he suggests, now operates mainly in, with and for the structures of the Church. This is precisely what gives chaplaincy its sharp distinctiveness as a genre of ministry: its situation within the structures of the wider society, whether hospital, prison, regiment, school, university, shopping centre, football club or other societal context.

The primary reason for a chaplain's being in any context is for him or her to be a 'Christian presence' within that (associational rather than local) community, suggests Ballard. While sharing the life of that community, the chaplain points beyond it, having a core loyalty to the person of Christ and to the values and teaching of the Church, which he or she seeks to relate and apply to the life of the community. And this is a missional vocation, rather than a simply evangelistic one; it isn't first and foremost about increasing the numbers of confessing Christians. Instead of seeking to gather a 'church' from within the working context, the chaplain is called to witness to Christ as the truth of God in the world. It is also a prophetic ministry, in which the chaplain is called to shed meaning and light and to be 'a positive presence, representing the possibility of hope and change'. Like those they work among, chaplains are caught up in the tension of the 'now' and 'not yet' of the Kingdom of God, the missional task being to discern what makes for the coming of the Kingdom for which we pray, and to work alongside others for its coming (Ballard 2009, pp.21–23).

The chaplain can also be seen as an interpreter, one who seeks to negotiate between the worldview of the ministerial context, its values and assumptions, and the spiritual vision of the Church. Community theologian Ann Morisy has explored this intermediary, interpretive role of chaplaincy and suggests that chaplains can 'open the conversation of Spirit' with those beyond the Church who do not share its spiritual awareness and who do not have access to the 'symbolic understandings' that link us to the transcendent. So the chaplain 'develop[s] the skill of code-switching'; that is, shifting between the language and symbolism of faith and that of every day. The chaplain 'works at the level of the imagination', to help people see beyond the routine and discover that 'within our ordinary experiences there are rumours of angels and traces of ultimacy' (Morisy 2006, p.153). This is a ministry of awakening, helping people become aware of the spiritual dimension and of the possibility of God.

As an interpreter of life's experiences, awakening others to the spiritual, the chaplain's role – whether or not he or she is ordained – is essentially and definitively priestly, helping bridge the gap between earth and heaven, using imagination and sensitivity to work alongside and with others. Embodying a spiritual vision, the chaplain is involved in the process of 're-enchanting' people's view of the world, helping them explore their sense of there being more to life than meets the eye, helping them interpret their own experiences in the light of the spiritual. Chaplaincy is about 'being priest for the everyday...representing, and occasionally speaking about, God's alongsideness in relation to daily life – whether the moment is filled with delight, stress or struggle' (Morisy 2006, p.129). It is this sense of being alongside people in the midst of their daily lives, sharing both their working context and the issues they face, that chaplains relish: seeking and finding Christ in the everyday, the Christ who calls us all to live in the light of the coming Kingdom.

Chaplaincy – locating the Church in the midst of society

This vision of chaplaincy is one which places it – and thus the Church which chaplains represent – in the very midst of society, rather than at its margins. I noted earlier Martyn Percy's view that 'ministries must engage with people', and – writing of a parish church – that a church 'must find a community and locate itself within it' (see p.125). It is essential to the nature of ministry both that it engages with people, and that it finds that engagement within the community in which it is located. Once we begin to see 'community' as a concept that may include but certainly extends beyond locality, it is clear that 'a Christian presence in every community' is a vision for the Church of England that can simply no longer be achieved solely on the basis of locality or of parochial ministry.

Rather, the Church now needs a vision that sees ministry extending throughout the complex range of interlocking, associational communities that form the wider community of the nation: all of these come under the heading of 'every natural community', which former Archbishop Rowan Williams sees as the proper sphere of ministry. If the Church's ministry is set within the midst of the community – the nation – in this sense, genuinely engaging with the national community about its concerns and aspirations, then there is a real chance of opening up for the wider society a vision of the Christ of every day. Public theology – the direct engagement with public and community issues from the Church's standpoint – becomes a priority, and chaplains are, as Ballard suggests, 'pivotal public theologians'. And it is in the varying and widespread contexts of chaplaincy – as well as in the traditional location of the parish – that the Church needs to be 'finding its places in society again' (Percy 2006, p.15).

The realisation that complex, modern societies comprise a web of interconnected and overlapping 'communities' of place, activity and interest is one that prompts us to have a vision of ministry broader than that offered by the impulse behind *Mission-Shaped Church* and its subsequent re-emergence in the 'Renewal and Reform' agenda. 'Inherited church', perceived as the dead hand of traditionalism by more radical voices, has in fact ensured the preservation and continuity of Christian presence, worship and ministry, and to dismiss it is to be in danger of abandoning the distinctive way in which the Christian faith has been shared and perpetuated in the context of English history and culture. To this extent, the inheritance of traditional structures – including the institutional forms of parish, church and vicar – is one that, as the authors of *For the Parish* insist, could be jettisoned only with dire consequences for the future of Christian faith in England.

The unexplored potential of worker-priest ministry

But there are further dimensions beyond those of parochial and chaplaincy ministry. A truly comprehensive vision for ministry in the Church of England of the future would not only encompass a continuing (if reduced) 'traditional' parish ministry alongside a developing variety of authorised chaplaincies, but also recognise the special nature and contribution of worker-priest ministry. Originating in a French Catholic movement of the 1950s, and beginning in the Southwark diocese in the early 1960s, worker-priest ministry has gone under a number of titles: auxiliary pastoral ministry (APM), non-stipendiary ministry (NSM), self-supporting ministry (SSM) and ministry in secular employment (MSE). The very variety of nomenclature expresses tellingly the Church's uncertainty about the nature and purpose of this ministry, and its potential remains severely undeveloped.

But worker-priest ministry, despite the Church's uncertainty, is in its essential conceptual nature close to chaplaincy: the associational community of the workplace is the sphere of mission and ministry, the worker-priest representing the Church in an officially recognised capacity. However, instead of being conceived in this way, worker-priest ministry has generally and reductively been seen as a usefully cost-free way of providing additional support to parish ministry, so that worker-priests have been deployed as parish curates, juniors in a hierarchical system of ordained parochial ministry, whose own ministerial and pastoral outreach in the workplace has been overlooked – much as chaplaincy has tended to be overlooked in a focus on the traditional Church and its pre-occupation with parish.

Worker-priest ministry has, again like chaplaincy, been seen as 'on the margins': a deeply ambiguous position. Chaplains speak of the rewards of liminality – being at the very edge of the Church and thus in a place of interaction with the wider world. And yet, liminality may mean being marginalised by the Church, as Steven Croft (2013) has recognised. Highlighting the key characteristics of worker-priest ministry as 'generosity, humility, liminality', he spoke in a sermon marking the 50th anniversary of the first Southwark worker-priest ordinations of the difficulty of living 'between two worlds'. Arguing that worker-priests should be properly supported by the traditional, structural institutions of bishops and dioceses, he talked about the importance of sustaining 'this edgy and liminal pattern of priesthood which is so vital for God's mission'.

Croft also noted the Church's need to develop its patterns of ministry – its need to ensure that priests working in different ministries are equally valued, and the financial limitations which, realistically, have to govern future planning:

> We will see the patterns continue to change and evolve in the next fifty years...more and more we will lose the distinction between priests who are stipendiary and priests who are self-supporting. I hope that all of us will learn to be generous, to be humble, to be liminal. I hope that we will grow a single

ministerial priesthood in which some of us, for some of our lives, receive financial support. (Croft 2013)

There is something singularly prophetic about this. But when we return to the current strategies of the Church of England at national level, we find little recognition, even, of the distinctive missional significance of chaplaincy, and even less of the potential of worker-priest ministry. So what pattern for the future might we envisage?

Engaging with society: in and beyond traditional structures

The English landscape speaks of the Christian past of the nation, and the institutions of parish and vicar retain resonance. 'Inherited church' is where we have come from, because Christian faith is continuous through history, a 'chain of memory' (Hervieu-Léger 2000) whose identity is perpetuated through all its acts of worship and commemoration, but most centrally through the sacraments of Baptism and Eucharist. The nation's churches – the places where these sacraments have been celebrated and where people have gathered over the ages to pray – remain a hugely significant part of the national inheritance of faith, even though the cost of maintenance may be unduly oppressive for small congregations in an age when active Christian affiliation is so slender. Inheritance is both gift and responsibility, cause for both gratitude and care. So, given the reality that 'communities' are geographical *and* associational, and that the parish is no longer the sole place where lives are located, the strategic challenge for the Church is to find the best way of maintaining the core of its parish-based ministry while actively developing its chaplaincy and worker-priest ministries within the networks and associations of wider society.

There are some hopeful signs that ways are being found to rethink how we use the inheritance of church buildings:

diversifying the functions of the local church building; developing the facility it offers; opening it up for more community use; designating 'festival' churches for occasional use only; taking out of use buildings that are no longer needed and conserving them as part of the national cultural heritage. Already some 350 church buildings have been handed into the care of The Churches Conservation Trust. Equally, there are hopeful signs that the traditional pattern of parochial ministry is being creatively adapted to provide a more flexible model responsive to new need and opportunity – though the complexities of some proffered solutions to adapting the Church's legal framework for ministry are frankly mind-boggling (see Church Commissioners 2010).

And change can be slow in the Church. It was argued almost 20 years ago that despite an increasing awareness of the need to diversify patterns of ministry, there has been an equally constant tendency to revert to the simplicity of the traditional model, characterised in the statement: 'Foster more vocations and grow congregations in our parish churches' (Williams 1998). The current 'Renewal and Reform' initiative could be heading in just this direction. An emphasis on seeking more vocations to professional parochial ministry and more church growth suggests that when thinking about ministry, the Church is unable to see or think outside the 'traditional structures' box, but this is understandable, since parish and vicar and church are what we have inherited.

What I am arguing here is that we should continue to honour the inherited parish ministry of locality, though accepting its limited reach into contemporary society. Hence, parochial ministry in the future should be on a necessarily reduced basis. 'A priest in every parish' has always been an unreachable ambition, and even 'a priest in every benefice' now looks unsustainable. The aim might be, therefore, 'a professional priest in every locality', where the definition of 'locality' will vary widely from town to city to suburb to country. One fruitful way of institutionalising this kind of approach is to look at the potential of the 'minster model' of ministry, where a single church in an area is designated as the resource centre for local mission and ministry. But part of this honouring of locality should be the understanding that the ministry of a paid, professional priest must be complemented by the ministry of others – of locally living worker-priests and chaplains, of lay ministers – who share an understanding of ministry as being by its nature essentially collaborative and diverse. But as well as honouring the traditional structures through which we have inherited the Church, its gospel and ministry, and recognising the continuing significance of local communities, we must first recognise and then act on the realisation that 'community' is not solely about locality, but also about association.

And it is in the associational communities of our society, those that make up the daily reality of life for most people in workplace, leisure centre, shopping mall and school, that there is the greatest opportunity for the Church's ministers and laypeople to engage with others as representatives of Christ and his Church. The varied ministries of chaplaincies – both the traditional 'institutional' chaplaincies of the health and prison services and of the armed forces, universities and schools, and the newer chaplaincies rooted in other associational communities (Slater 2015) – are, like worker-priests, at the very interface of Church and society. If we truly have a vision of mission that is broader and more profound than a focus on growth in numbers, and if we have a sense of the 'now and not yet' of the Kingdom of God, then we shall realise that chaplaincy and the work of priests in the workplace not only provide challenging paradigms for all ministry, but are where we need to see the frontier of the mission of the Church in this century.

References

Abbott, W.M. (ed.) (1966) *The Documents of Vatican II.* Piscataway, NJ: New Century Publishers Inc.

Avis, P. (2003) *A Church Drawing Near: Spirituality and Mission in a Post-Christian Culture.* London and New York: T&T Clark.

Avis, P. (2005) *A Ministry Shaped by Mission*. London and New York: T&T Clark.

Bailey, E. (1998) *Implicit Religion: An Introduction*. London: Middlesex University Press.

Ballard, P. (2009) 'Locating chaplaincy: a theological note.' *Crucible* July–September 2009: 18–24.

Caperon, J. (2015) *A Vital Ministry: Chaplaincy in Schools in the Post-Christian Era*. London: SCM Press.

Church Commissioners (2010) *Innovative and Unusual Pastoral Arrangements: Some Scenarios*. London: Church of England. Accessed on 7/7/2017 at: www.churchofengland.org/media/55265/innovativepastoralarrcontents.doc.

Church of England (2016) 'Renewal & Reform.' Accessed on 28/2/2017 at www.churchofengland.org/renewal-reform.aspx.

Cray, G. (2004) *Mission-Shaped Church: Church Planting and Fresh Expressions of Church in a Changing Context*. London: Church House Publishing.

Croft, S. (ed.) (2006) *The Future of the Parish System: Shaping the Church of England for the Twenty-First Century*. London: Church House Publishing.

Croft, S. (2013) 'A new pattern of priesthood.' Accessed on 7/7/2017 at: www.with-intent.confiteor.org.uk/steven-croft-southwark-ordination-cours-anniversary.html.

Davison, A. and A. Milbank (2010) *For the Parish: A Critique of Fresh Expressions*. London: SCM Press.

Hervieu-Léger, D. (2000) *Religion as a Chain of Memory*. Cambridge and Maldon, MA: Polity.

House of Bishops (2011) *Challenges for the New Quinquennium*. London: General Synod of the Church of England. Accessed on 7/7/2017 at: www.churchofengland.org/media/1163101/gs%201815.pdf.

Hull, J. (2006) *Mission-Shaped Church: A Theological Response*. London: SCM Press.

MacCulloch, D. (2009) *A History of Christianity: The First Three Thousand Years*. London: Allen Lane.

Morisy, A. (2006) 'Mapping the Mixed Economy.' In S. Croft *The Future of the Parish System*. London: Church House Publishing.

Percy, M. (2006) 'Many Rooms in My Father's House: The Changing Identity of the English Parish Church.' In S. Croft *The Future of the Parish System*. London: Church House Publishing.

Percy, M. (2016) 'On not rearranging the deckchairs on the titanic: A commentary on reform and renewal in the Church of England.' *Modern Church*. Accessed on 7/7/2017 at: http://modernchurch.org.uk/downloads/finish/818-articles/768-on-not-rearranging-the-deckchairs-on-the-titanic.

Rahner, K. (1963) *Mission and Grace*. London and New York: Sheed and Ward.

Ryan, B. (2015) *A Very Modern Ministry: Chaplaincy in the UK*. London: Theos.

Slater, V. (2015) *Chaplaincy Ministry and the Church of England*. London: SCM Press.

Spencer, S. (2015) 'Goals for growth expose a vision's limitations.' *Church Times*. 14 August 2015. Available at: www.churchtimes.co.uk/articles/2015/14-august/comment/opinion/goals-for-growth-expose-a-vision-s-limitations.

Westcott House (2013) '"Ministry where people are": a view of chaplaincy.' *Westcott House: 2012–2013 the year in Review 2012–2013*.

Williams, J.A. (1998) 'Towards diversity: renewing the church's ministry.' *Anvil* 15(1): 41–51. Accessed on 7/7/2017 at: https://biblicalstudies.org.uk/pdf/anvil/15-1_041.pdf.

Williams, R. (2006) 'Theological Resources for Re-examining Church.' In S. Croft *The Future of the Parish System*. London: Church House Publishing.

7

CHAPLAINCY AND EVANGELISM
— JAMES WALTERS AND CHARLOTTE BRADLEY —

Is chaplaincy just decoration?

'First, the Church exists to worship God in Jesus Christ. Second, the Church exists to make new disciples of Jesus Christ. Everything else is decoration' (Welby 2015). The Church of England has woken up to the need for evangelism. The twentieth century saw a very slow but persistent decline in church attendance, the impact of which, particularly among younger people, is now revealing its full effect. An 81-year-old is eight times more likely than a 21-year-old to attend church. To speak of a demographic time bomb is too dramatic. The decline has been gradual and sustained, but we are only now waking up to its scale. Furthermore, if unaddressed, this decline is set to continue for another three decades. Few people now attend church out of family expectation or social pressure. The Church cannot simply wait for new members to come through its doors. People need to hear the invitation of Christ to be part of his Church.

Hence the Archbishop of Canterbury's identification of evangelism as one of his three key priorities as he took up office. He rightly stresses that, 'evangelism is not a growth strategy' (Welby 2015). Yet it must be said that the Renewal and Reform programme he has initiated, which is freeing up money for missional initiatives, is shaking the Church out of the complacency that we can always occupy a central place in British society when an ever-shrinking proportion of the British population believe what we believe and participate in what we do. There is a sense of urgency around and an awareness that if evangelism is not taken more seriously by the whole Church, then we simply will not have the numbers in the future to sustain our current activity or legitimise our unusually privileged established status.

So if the Church exists to worship and evangelise, as Archbishop Justin suggests, where does chaplaincy fit in? Is it mere decoration? Are chaplains the legacy of an age when the Church was part of the furniture of British society with resources to spend on this kind of public presence? In this chapter, we will explore the relationship of chaplaincy to the present climate of 'intentional evangelism'. We will inevitably focus on the issues raised by the chaplaincy context in which we operate – higher education – but we believe these insights will have parallels and address similar challenges in other sectors.

We begin with the assumption that evangelism is integral to all Christian witness and that chaplaincy is no exception. It is certainly the case that Christian ministry should not be instrumentalised for growth. We should not preach the gospel of Jesus or further his Kingdom in the world for any reason other than that we have been commanded to do so and to glorify God. It may well be that the Church should minister at times and in contexts where there is no possibility of any kind of missionary success, but that is not the argument of this chapter. We take it as read that chaplaincy exercised well leads to the numerical growth of disciples and that an investment in chaplaincy is an investment in the future of the Church. But there are a number of considerations and sensitivities involved, particularly in the secular and multi-faith environments in which chaplains work. So the argument of this chapter will be threefold. First, we will explore the complex sensitivities involved in chaplaincy within these contexts and consider the ways in which this ministry contributes to the missionary activity of the whole Church. These sensitivities may mean that explicit evangelism is not the primary focus of the chaplain's ministry, but that is not to say chaplains are not contributing to the evangelistic mission of the Church. Second, we will set out what we have found to be the necessary conditions of intentional evangelism within the secular/multi-faith environment in which we operate. Third, we will set out how we think chaplains might more appropriately be leaders in mission rather than lone evangelists. We hope to demonstrate that within the ecology of the Church's mission – including the growth in number of disciples – chaplaincy is far from decorative!

Building up the Body

The gifts he gave were that some would be apostles, some prophets, some evangelists, some pastors and teachers, to equip the saints for the work of ministry, for building up the body of Christ, until all of us come to the unity of the faith and of the knowledge of the Son of God, to maturity, to the measure of the full stature of Christ.

(Ephesians 4.11–13)

The identification of 'evangelist' as one of a number of gifts given by Christ to the Church has led some to believe that evangelism is the calling of only some Christians. Archbishop Justin disagrees, seeing evangelism as rooted 'in the life and witness of every Christian – not only the professionals' (Welby 2015). Muddiman's interpretation of Ephesians lends this view some credence in that he sees the author as identifying two focuses of ministry: preaching the gospel and caring for Christ's flock. He suggests that the second couplet – evangelists and pastors – is an interpretation of the earlier roles of the apostles and prophets. But he also believes that the author 'was flexible about the actual titles by which these activities could be duly recognised in the Church'

(Muddiman 2001, p.199). There is some cause, therefore, to see these titles as emphases of ministry rather than exclusive job descriptions. One may have a pastoral focus but still share in the work of evangelism, and vice versa. This reflects how these different facets of ministry have been incorporated into each of the sacred ministries within the threefold order of the Church of England. The priest is to 'lead Christ's people in proclaiming his glorious gospel, so that the good news of salvation may be heard in every place'. She is also to 'faithfully minister the doctrine and sacraments of Christ...so that the people committed to [her] charge may be defended against error and flourish in the faith' (Common Worship, *The Ordination of Priests, also called Presbyters*).

There is some mileage in equating a chaplain with being the parish priest of that institution. Part of a chaplain's role is to be the glue that holds the institutional community together in the same way that a parish priest is expected to be a community leader, particularly in times of celebration or grief in the life of the institution. The chaplain is often the first port of call for deaths (as well as births and marriages, although these are less common among an undergraduate population at least); most chaplains have oversight of a chapel or space used for faith groups and are expected to manage the design and usage of the space in the same way a parish priest would manage his or her church. But there are some who would argue that this comparison only goes so far. In their research into student Christianity, Guest *et al.* suggest:

> The model of the parish priest is no longer an obvious or adequate template for priests working in contemporary university contexts. Chaplaincy has become a site for innovation and experiment in public and plural faith, a focus of adaptation as chaplains reach out to those beyond the normal boundaries of the church. (Guest *et al.* 2013, p.142)

However, this reaching out to those 'beyond the normal boundaries of the church' is something many parish priests are and should equally be engaging in. We, therefore, wish to interpret the chaplain's ministry in the same way as that of any priest ordained in the Church of England – that of a multifaceted ministry in which different gifts are required with different emphasis at different times.

It is true to say that the evangelistic ministry is often not the primary focus of chaplaincy, and for very good reasons.

- *Secular* institutions may recognise the pastoral value of chaplaincy but be wary of any particular religious views being promoted. This may be for reasons of equality or a feeling that the institution has no interest in promoting any religious view at all. Chaplains need to be acutely aware of this concern where the secular institution is the key funder.

- Within the *multi-faith* context, chaplains need to be aware of the sensitivities of other religious groups. Particular sensitivity may need to be shown to groups that have historically been subject to forcible conversion to Christianity, like the Jewish people.

- Misconceptions about coercive proselytism may also discourage non-Christians from accessing chaplaincy services if they develop a strong reputation for evangelistic intent. Some evangelistic reserve can therefore be a *pastoral* sensitivity.

Chaplains who are employed by a secular institution therefore have to be more aware of how their calling as evangelists might be perceived than most parish priests might. We will explore how we have addressed some of these sensitivities in more depth in the next section. But at this stage, two things need to be said about, what we might call, 'evangelistic reticence' in chaplaincy.

First, while the shift in the Church toward 'intentional evangelism' is undoubtedly a positive move in developing the confidence of all people in speaking more openly about their faith, 'intentional' should not always be taken to mean 'overt'. Many chaplains experience opportunities to talk and pray with people as they arise naturally in the course of their ministries. Furthermore, the evangelistic witness of the chaplain should not be reduced to these kinds of conversation alone. This is where the complex question of metrics is raised. How do we measure evangelistic impact and church growth? This question is not merely hypothetical. In allocating resources from the Strategic Development Fund, the Church Commissioners and Archbishops' Council are understandably looking for discernable impact and measurable outcomes. But we need to be careful about making too reductionist an assessment. Should we really only measure evangelistic impact in terms of the number of non-Christians brought to baptism by a chaplain? Chaplains are in the business of building the credibility of the Church within the secular world, and that building of credibility and trust takes time. Particularly in schools and universities, the chaplain may be sowing seeds of future faith or indeed watering the seeds others have sown, without yet reaping the harvest. As St Paul says, 'I planted, Apollos watered, but God was causing the growth' (1 Corinthians 3.6). We can never know if a positive experience of chaplaincy contributes significantly to a future step of faith.

This leads to the second consideration, which also returns us to the passage from Ephesians. Evangelism may be a responsibility of all Christians but the role is differentiated here within a passage that draws attention to how the whole Church of diverse gifts works together. No chaplain is a 'lone ranger' but works with all the saints to build all people up to the full stature of Christ. It is unlikely to be the case that the chaplain is the only Christian presence within an institution and it may be that part of the chaplain's role is enabling other kinds of Christian witness to take place. Regrettably, there has developed over many years a destructive culture of hostility between some university chaplains and some student mission organisations. While there are encouraging exceptions, in many places chaplains can be branded as 'gatekeepers' and seen as an obstacle rather than an enabler of mission. A culture of collaboration would be far more conducive to the growth of the Church in its diversity. Nothing is more damaging to the Church's mission than Christians at loggerheads, as Jesus tells us in the high priestly prayer of John's Gospel: '[I ask] that they may all be one. As you, Father, are in me and I am in you, may they also be in us, so that the world may believe' (John 17.21). Secular institutions do look to chaplains to take a gatekeeper role, which is crucial in the face of the destructive forms of religion that would seek to exploit young people. Yet gatekeepers can hold doors open as well as close them, and in many cases the chaplain is holding a space open within a highly suspicious secular environment, which enables evangelistic activity to take place. There is an urgent need for a greater appreciation of the mutual dependence of these members of the ecclesial body to see how God is working among us as 'Pauls' and 'Apolloses' to increase the unity of faith and knowledge of the Son of God.

Getting more intentional

The previous section has set out some possible reasons why chaplains may be reticent about overt evangelism and feel undervalued in a culture that focuses too exclusively on church growth. We maintain, however, that more intentional evangelistic initiatives are both possible and appropriate given the right circumstances and institutional trust. In September 2016, we launched a new worshipping community for students across higher education institutions in London, which meets on Sunday evenings and is called The Anchorage.

Substantial preparation was given to considering the kind of missional initiative appropriate to our context and building a story around it. The name, for example, alludes to the description of Christian hope in the Letter to the Hebrews as 'a sure and steadfast anchor of the soul' (Hebrews 6.19). But it also connects us to the local parish of St Clement Dane, whose symbol is the anchor and whose vicarage was called The Anchorage and was part of the LSE campus until its demolition. We have also given a lot of thought to the life of the community itself and how it responds to the needs of the particular London student constituency. The Anchorage centres around four key values:

- *Building community.* Universities are seeing a rise in mental health difficulties in students. This is often caused by a toxic mixture of a demanding workload, familial pressure to succeed academically, the financial burden that university fees and living costs entails, and a difficulty in forming friendships. London can be a particularly isolating place for students and as such we wanted to build a supportive community where we give time to listening to each other and welcoming newcomers.

- *Faithful enquiry.* Both of us had had numerous encounters with students who wanted to engage intellectually with their Christian faith but weren't being encouraged to do so or didn't know where to start. We wanted to give students the opportunity to critically engage with and discuss their faith in the same manner that they would do with their studies.

- *Signs of grace.* Every week we lead an act of worship to enable a sacramental encounter with God. This may include the Eucharist, foot washing, anointing or Ignatian meditation.

- *Acts of mercy.* The danger of a non-parochial church community is that it could become focused solely on the needs of its members. We have encouraged students to take part in local church outreach projects such as a soup kitchen, youth group and interfaith initiatives. We actively promote a view of discipleship as a life of service.

Launching this initiative has involved navigating a number of sensitivities, which we will now set out as theoretical conditions for mission in a secular institution.

Building trust

Religion is a source of contention in much of the world today and particularly in British society. Within our own institutions (secular universities) all kinds of historic prejudices about religion as anti-intellectual and socially conservative are meeting new concerns about the radicalisation of students and campus divisions that appear to run along religious fault lines. The religious identity of students frequently generates confusion and anxiety among university leaders and we have found our institutions looking to us to help them navigate complexities they do not understand and to foster relationships across religious groups. They might not have readily understood in the early stages that it could be possible to do this while, at the same time, representing our own faith, including being evangelists. To do this, therefore, requires the building of trust over time. We had been working in our institutions for six and three years respectively before discerning that it would be possible to complement our existing chaplaincy activities with an intentionally evangelistic initiative. To have attempted it sooner might have undermined our positions and the fragile relationships between our institutions and the church, which have been delicately negotiated over many years. If secular institutions are not to reject evangelism then they must have learned to trust those who are doing it, and this takes time.

Delineating proselytism from evangelism

They may not always realise it, but chaplains are in privileged positions of power. They represent institutions (hospitals, prisons, schools) that have varying degrees of control and influence over people, which is to say nothing of the spiritual power invested in the institution of the Church. This makes it even more important, therefore, that consideration is given to the often fine line between proselytism and evangelism. When does telling somebody about your faith become an inappropriate assertion of influence? In our context, for example, it would be wholly inappropriate to suggest to a troubled student who had come to see us for support that the answer to their problems was conversion to the Christian faith, without some explicit prompting on their part. That kind of conversation, if it were to be welcomed, would have to take place in a more established relationship where the chaplain could not be accused of exploiting either institutional privilege or the student's distress in order to 'recruit new Christians'.

There may be no hard and fast rules about this and there will certainly remain those in the university who believe that any promotion of religion is an unacceptable form of proselytism. Universities are, however, required by law to uphold freedom of speech and we consider it to be of utmost importance that religion is accepted as part of the free market of ideas the university is expected to be. Part of the chaplain's role is to advocate for this and ensure that nervousness about religion does not lead to an unacceptable exclusion of religious expression from the campus. The Equality Act 2010 requires that religion and belief are treated in this way. Socialist ideas are promoted in universities in the hope that students will become socialists. Capitalist ideas are promoted in the hope that students will become capitalists. There is absolutely no reason why Christianity should not be promoted in the hope that students will become Christians.

Establishing boundaries

Just as the letter to the Ephesians differentiates between the charisms of evangelist and pastor, so we have found it helpful to establish boundaries around aspects of our chaplaincy work. The aspects of our work that fall under the category of pastor would include our role as brokers of interfaith dialogue on diverse campuses and obviously in counselling students of all faiths and none. An example of the pastoral boundary with vulnerable students is given above. As an example of boundaries in interfaith work, we would not proactively invite a student of another faith to attend The Anchorage. But we have certainly not turned away those who have heard about it and come along or been brought by their friends. We also seek to promote a model of interfaith engagement that allows people who hold exclusivist religious beliefs to be able to discuss them. Interfaith dialogue should not lead to syncretism, and committed students of other faiths have been appreciative of our honesty when we have said that as Christian priests we would ultimately like to see others sharing our beliefs. But these kinds of conversation can only take place once trust has been established, particularly trust that as chaplain to the whole student body you will advocate on behalf of other faith traditions and support them in their religious observance.

Maintaining the right boundaries has been helped in our case by the fact that our universities operate primarily from Monday to Friday, enabling us to adopt the more explicitly evangelistic role when The Anchorage meets on Sundays.

Connecting with the wider church

While one of us is substantially funded by the university and the other is funded entirely by the Church, we both remain diocesan priests and our chaplaincy posts represent a partnership between secular universities and the Church of England. This has helped us to locate this new initiative within the mission objectives of the diocese and to build a network of supporters, both practical and in prayer. We have had support from local clergy, their pastoral assistants, the diocesan team, and from bishops. We also benefited enormously from the diocesan church-planting course, which seeks to prepare church leaders who are planning to plant a new congregation or substantial new development within their current church. This wider network has greatly assisted us in developing the evangelistic dimensions of our chaplaincy ministries.

Chaplains frequently talk about isolation in their ministry and we have found that engaging in this missional initiative has been both supportive to us in the roles we play outside the church, as well as furthering the interests of church growth.

Space and resourcing

The final condition for this new mission initiative has been the practical considerations of a suitable, accessible space and the resources we received to get a new worshipping community off the ground. Many chaplains, particularly in secular situations, have inadequate space for Christian gatherings. This is where chaplains need to be alert to the conversations that many public institutions are having about Islamic prayer space and ensure that properly inclusive arrangements are put in place that allow religious observance across the board, and not just the most obvious, pressing need. In addition to the practicalities of the venue, the space we use to meet is located within a student centre building where there is also a bar, gym, cafe, work spaces – i.e. the kind of space where students spend a lot of time. It can be easy for many of us to become so accustomed to church environments that it is difficult to sympathise with the intimidating connotations that many churches have for those who don't frequent them. Financial resource is also essential, and as dioceses review all expenditure (including chaplaincy) we welcome the changing climate that is prepared to put money into well-thought-through mission initiatives.

Chaplains as leaders in mission

Much of this chapter has been considering how chaplains can balance different roles within themselves and view evangelism as compatible with each of those roles. Our final reflections, however, are on how we think chaplains can enable others to be evangelists. There are two reasons for focusing on this. The first is that while we have argued that evangelism should be seen as one facet of the chaplain's ministry (as it should be for all clergy), we are also clear that it cannot be the primary focus for those of us who work in secular institutions. Our universities will mainly want to see us responding to the initiatives of the student body rather than imposing our own agenda. It has been essential, therefore, that The Anchorage has had strong student leadership from the start and that a core team of students is responsible for the front-line evangelistic interaction with their peers. We view our roles as chaplains in this area to be primarily that of leading others in mission.

The second reason is to challenge aspects of a wider culture of church growth that appear to place a heavy and sole emphasis on transformational leaders. Martyn Percy has condemned this as the rise of the 'executive mission-minded-middle-manager' paradigm geared more towards narrowly construed organisational growth than to the development of the Church as a complex social institution (Percy 2014). Cultivating leadership in the right ways is clearly crucial to the growth of the Church. But we view our leadership of The Anchorage as primarily about raising up the leadership of others, particularly as evangelists. It may be that today's emphasis on mission-focused leadership is a new version of the clericalism that has so often held back gifted and willing laypeople. An alumnus of one of our institutions was a lay theologian who was particularly insistent on the point that the diversity of the Church's ministries should not all be located within the priest. William Stringfellow, who studied at the LSE in the late 1940s, wrote:

> That a priest was in any sense more exalted than any other person, in the life of the gospel in the world, could not be true. And if a priest were that in the life of the church, then it could only betray something profoundly false in the church. (Stringfellow 1994, p.27)

So, if it is impossible to resolve all the evangelist/pastor tensions within the person of the chaplain, we believe it is possible to do so if chaplaincy is not conceived of as isolated individuals, but rather as ministers connected to the wider church and leading Christian community (however small) within their contexts. Even within secular institutions, therefore, the chaplain is engaged in the building up of what Daniel Hardy described as 'godly sociality'. It is this sociality that is the essence of the Church and, Hardy suggests, it cannot 'be itself without moving, both within itself and with others: it is mission-constituted' (Hardy 2001, p.40). We see the evangelistic ministry of chaplains not so much as street preachers on soapboxes but rather as inextricably linked to the animating of this dynamic community. They operate within the constraints of secular institutions that often have profound anxieties about the presence of religion. Yet it has been our experience that as trust and understanding develop, there is a recognition that it is precisely in the chaplain's full capacities as a religious leader (both pastor and evangelist) that they are of most benefit to their institution in caring for students of all faiths and none, and in helping them navigate the choppy waters of religion in the public square today.

References

Guest, M., Aune, K., Sharma, S. and Warner, R. (2013) *Christianity and the University Experience: Understanding Student Faith.* London: Bloomsbury.

Hardy, D.W. (2001) *Finding the Church.* London: SCM Press.

Percy, M. (2014) 'Are these the leaders that we really want?' *Church Times,* 12 December 2014.

Muddiman, J. (2001) *The Epistle to the Ephesians.* London: Continuum.

Stringfellow, W. (1994) *A Keeper of the Word.* Grand Rapids: Eerdmans.

Welby, J. (2015) Inaugural Lambeth Lecture. Accessed on 7/7/2017 at: www.archbishopofcanterbury.org/articles.php/5515/lambeth-lectures-archbishop-justin-on-evangelism-video.

8

CONCLUSION
An Invitation to Theology
ANDREW TODD

Introduction

The major thread through this book has been theological reflection rooted in the contemporary practice of chaplaincy in different settings. Rather than offering a definitive theology, missiology or ecclesiology, chaplaincy invites reflection in those areas and offers contextual responses. However, a consistent feature of those responses is that they emerge from a practice that exists in multiple social domains, and that crosses boundaries between those domains. Chaplaincy occasions, therefore, theology that also crosses boundaries, and that arises out of the dialogue, negotiation and even contestation between domains. This kind of theology, almost as a matter of necessity, involves re-envisaging theology (and missiology and ecclesiology).

Reconceiving 'religion'

Meredith McGuire in her book, *Lived Religion* (2008), provides an interesting analogy for this relocation of theology. A significant aspect of her book acts as an invitation to sociologists of religion to rethink what they understand by that term, 'religion'. She sets out this part of her agenda thus:

> I examine four issues that, I believe, are particularly important for understanding that what scholars nowadays

think of as definitive of 'real' religion and religious action is itself a social construction, the result of human struggles over cultural resources and power:

The location of the sacred...

The nature of divine power...

The focus of individual religious expression...

The purity and authenticity of religious tradition and group identity...

Recognizing that these definitional boundaries are social constructions does not mean we must discard the concepts, but does require us to realize that the resulting distinctions are not inherent properties of 'religion' or 'the sacred'. (McGuire 2008, pp.21–22)

In the sections that follow, McGuire reviews a range of scholarship that suggests that late-medieval religion was characterised by diversity; localism; eclecticism; the social pervasiveness of sacred space and time; and the reality of sacred power (located in different people, rites and symbols across social groups) (McGuire 2008, pp.25–32). McGuire contrasts this with religion as it was restructured in the 'Long Reformation' (c.1400–1700), which affected not only protestant and reformed churches, but also the Catholic Church. She proposes that this restructuring involved: a move to emphasise belief over practice; a relocation of sacred power (significantly within the hands of religious leaders, rather than more widely); the suppression of 'magic'; and standardisation, in order to exercise control over eclecticism, diversity and the local. She concludes:

In all of the aforementioned cultural and political contests of meaning, the winners were those who could set the terms of discourse for the others: the courtly mannered elites defining propriety; leaders of religious sects setting the terms for who would be accepted into their membership as religiously qualified; the inquisitors and religious judges defining orthodoxy (correct belief) and orthopraxy (correct practice); the bishops and higher clergy centralizing their control over practices in the hinterlands; regional religiopolitical powers centralizing their control over previously autonomous towns and city-states, and so on. (McGuire 2008, p.43)

The point that arises out of this historicising of the study of religion is that sociologists today commonly work with a construction of religion that owes much to, and indeed emerged in, the 'Long Reformation' period; a construction that focuses on religion as boundaried, institutional and subject to religious authorities. They do this rather than work with a construct drawn from earlier periods, in which religion may have been much less of a distinct entity and much more something that pervaded social life. This in turn shapes scholars' view of religion today, with particular consequences. Thus, if we focus on religion today as: defined and controlled by institutions; standardised around dominant beliefs; differentiated as the sacred, over and against the profane; and as a distinct domain within the secular state; then we are likely to see mainly (or only) a picture of decline in the twentieth and twenty-first centuries. This would, in part, account for the prominence of the 'secularisation' debate within the sociology of religion in that period. If, however, we focus on 'lived religion', a different picture will emerge. So, for example, McGuire asks:

Rather than take the notion of a clear sacred-profane dichotomy for granted as a defining feature of religion, what would we understand about individuals' religious lives – now, as well as four centuries ago – if we considered the possibility that some, perhaps many, religious persons experience the sacred as arising *within* the profane world? (2008, p.32)

Much of the rest of her book works with such alternative constructions of religion, revealing a diversity of practice characterised by the richness and authority of people's own experience (as well as that of religious institutions and organisations); where religious practice may be declining in some places, but flourishing in others. The picture that emerges includes aspects of institutional religion, but also religious practice that overflows, and contests, institutional boundaries.

Chaplaincy similarly acts as an invitation to rethink what we mean by 'religion' today. Chaplains also come across what McGuire describes as 'lived religion'. This comes in different forms and from different people, including those disenchanted by institutional religion, as well as those who have little or no experience or knowledge of established faith organisations. Chaplains encounter those wrestling with what is sacred in their lives, and how to mark that in ritual ways, in acute settings such as healthcare, prisons and military operations, and in more everyday settings like the workplace, town centres, the retail industry and education. Chaplains also embody, encounter and enable expressions of institutional religion (church life, for example), but in settings outside religious domains (in Christian terms, away from church buildings and the gathered life of the Church within them).

Further, chaplains frequently engage with religion, both formal and informal, as it is shaped and relocated by public norms, or secular sacralities (see Pattison 2015). This book was developed from a public context in the UK in which one particularly significant aspect of this is the emergence of 'spirituality' as a parallel construct to 'religion'. In relation, for example, to spiritual care in healthcare, spirituality acts as an accommodating discourse, embracing those aspects of religion and belief that are useful within the public sphere, or amenable to its norms of respect for diversity, or public safety, while constraining versions of religion that are less 'safe'.

This shaping of religion within mainstream public life has the additional effect of bringing together, sometimes in one particular place (such as a public institution), wide-ranging religious practices and forms. This includes the bringing together of: different world faiths in the setting of multi-faith chaplaincy; traditional liturgical forms and informal liturgy; those who are religious, or spiritual, or spiritual but not religious, or 'none of the above'.

It is little wonder, therefore, that chaplains often refer to themselves as 'liminal' people, a word that seems to capture the way that chaplaincy is practised in multiple social domains, sometimes in between those domains and often on and across their boundaries. Positioned thus, chaplains often negotiate between different forms of religion and between them and other dimensions of the diverse context (with managers of public institutions, for example), enabling significant dialogue, debate and boundary-crossing (as well as, on occasion, contesting of boundaries) for themselves and for those they serve.

Reconstructing 'theology'

The engagement that chaplaincy has with a breadth of religion, belief and spirituality, together with the 'liminal' role within that, has a corresponding effect on the way in which the construct 'theology' works for chaplains. Of necessity, they need a theology, or theologies, that can encompass the breadth of their experience of religion. That doesn't necessarily mean theology which is all-inclusive. I have heard recently from a small, but growing, number of chaplains working in different multi-faith contexts, words to the effect: 'I am not multi-anything!' This is not a refusal to engage with those of different faiths, nor does it mean that they won't work alongside chaplains of different faiths, or engage in dialogue with them. Rather, it seems to articulate that they do so out of the integrity of their own theological position, combined with a sensitivity to other viewpoints. Rowan Williams, in her chapter in this book, explores something of living with that tension.

It is out of just such theological wrestling that the chapters in this book arise, each offering a particular perspective on the resulting reflection. What this conclusion does, in order to complement the contextual approaches of each chapter, is to draw together the questions arising, and to offer them to all those involved in theological pondering on the Church's life, mission and ministry, within a complex and diverse society.

The first question arising is whether the Church's theology is wide enough in scope to enable chaplains and others to recognise and respond to the presence and action of God in diverse social domains – indeed in any social domain. Do we have a theological language(s) that can be drawn on in the public sphere – in civil society; in a society characterised by a diversity of belief and religious/spiritual practice; in relation to the different dimensions of people's lives within contemporary society (including work, leisure, unemployment, moments of crisis or isolation and family life as well as those aspects that might be recognised as explicitly or overtly 'religious)?

That question needs to be accompanied by a second one about whether such a theology enables people to deploy it in quite different social settings and on the boundaries between them, speaking from the institutional to the personal and *vice versa*; between the private and the public; in the midst of a dialogue of religions and beliefs; and further dialogue involving religious positions, speaking within domains characterised by different kinds of secularity. As I indicated in Chapter 1, this is also a question about what sources of theology contribute to this kind of theological repertoire. Further, the question is about whether, in the language of Cameron *et al.* (2010), theological voices that are normative (perhaps confessional) or formal (coming from an academic context) are brought into conversation with voices that emerge from particular situations. Those situational voices, in the language of Cameron *et al.*, may be espoused (articulated by those engaged in a situation), or operant (at work in the situation without necessarily being made explicit). A significant question emerging from this book, is whether among those espoused and operant voices are discerned the theological perspectives and theologically freighted practices of individuals from a wide range of belief positions, whose positions critique the normative and formal voices.

As different chapters have shown, the need for such theology to be robust and discerning requires reflection on the hermeneutics at work. For chaplains, but also for many other Christians, there is a question about how best to bring the Christian tradition into critical dialogue and correlation (cf. Browning 1996, pp.44–47; Tracy 1975, pp.43–63) with quite different contemporary viewpoints. How, for example, does Christian theology today correlate understanding of dignity rooted in the belief that people are created in the image of God, with other perspectives on dignity that highlight the importance of our being able to be rational autonomous agents (see Soulen and Woodhead 2006), especially when vital issues to do with beginning and end of life are under consideration? As part of the response to such questions, this book argues that robustness does not consist of steadfast adherence to just one view, but rests in the willingness to address difference. In the field of chaplaincy, this not infrequently requires those in dialogue to discover mediating languages, often that of contemporary ethics, with all parties translating their views into the in-between language as a way of bringing them into a common space.

The corollary of a robust theology with a generous scope is a missiology that is also not unduly constrained by ecclesiastical perspectives. This book focuses its missiological reflections in two ways. The first of these asks all those involved in Christian mission how seriously they take the

Bosch principle (1991), that mission is first and foremost something that has to do with the transformative presence and action of God (the *missio Dei*); and then that which the Church does to participate in God's mission.

This gives rise to the second missiological question, which is about how we understand the economy of mission. Within this area, a particular question is whether and how chaplains may be evangelistic, especially in public institutions that may be suspicious of religion, and of proselytisation in particular. A further question is about the valuing of other aspects of mission alongside evangelism, not least the pastoral care for which chaplaincy is often renowned. James Walters and Charlotte Bradley, from their experience as university chaplains, explore the particular tension between pastoral care and evangelism, arguing for an inclusive understanding of mission, but also for evangelism being one aspect of what chaplains do, often built on the trust that chaplains have established within their host organisations. In parallel with this reflection on evangelism and the relationship of trust between chaplains and those they serve, is Margaret Whipp's exploration of how Christian pastoral care can be exercised with integrity in the healthcare context, rather than as a Trojan Horse that hides a less than sensitive mission agenda. We also have Ben Ryan's timely plea for chaplaincy to focus particularly on its role of relationship building.

This book thus asks whether Christian mission is engaged with looking and listening for God's mission – with respecting and honouring the work that God does beyond the range of the Church's mission, as well as through it. It argues for an understanding of mission that includes this discerning dimension (and the need for dialogue as part of this), but places this alongside both the proclamation of God's transforming love and the celebration of that love within the gathered life of the Church.

In relocating and broadening the focus of theological reflection and missiology, the book also stretches understandings of ecclesiology. John Caperon explores chaplaincy alongside parish ministry, looking at how the Church can have a properly parochial approach to its engagement with the whole life of our society, drawing on complementary models of ministry. James Walters, in turn, deconstructs the way in which an overly polarised understanding of Church and world militates against an understanding of the Church as one, holy, catholic and apostolic that has, as he argues, the potential to structure and shape the Church's involvement in 'secular' society.

The book as a whole, therefore, offers practical theological reflections rooted in chaplaincy that invite all committed to the Christian theological enterprise to re-envisage, not only how they view contemporary religion, but also how they engage with theology, missiology and ecclesiology. Chaplaincy proposes a relocation. It does this through and out of its engagement with different social domains, its reaching across boundaries in order to serve people, and through the dialogue and relationship building with those of diverse backgrounds, beliefs and perspectives that enables such service within the public sphere and civil society. This relocation involves an understanding of religion, belief and spirituality that is not constrained by focusing solely on the institutional and on decline. It also involves the stretching of theological perspectives beyond organisational boundaries, so that they may embrace the full extent (in so far as we can perceive it) of God's transformative presence and action in the world today.

References

Bosch, D. (1991) *Transforming Mission: Paradigm Shifts in Theology of Mission*. New edition. Maryknoll, NY: Orbis Books.

Browning, D. S. (1996) *A Fundamental Practical Theology: Descriptive and Strategic Proposals*. Minneapolis: Fortress Press.

Cameron, H., Bhatti, D., Duce, C., Sweeney, J. and Watkins, C. (2010) *Talking About God in Practice: Theological Action Research and Practical Theology*. London: SCM Press.

McGuire, M.B. (2008) *Lived Religion: Faith and Practice in Everyday Life.* Oxford; New York: Oxford University Press.

Pattison, S. (2015) 'Situating Chaplaincy in the United Kingdom: The Acceptable Face of "Religion"?' In C. Swift, M. Cobb and A. Todd (eds) *A Handbook of Chaplaincy Studies: Understanding Spiritual Care in Public Places.* Ashgate Contemporary Ecclesiology. Aldershot and Burlington, VT: Ashgate.

Soulen, R.K. and Woodhead, L. (eds) (2006) *God and Human Dignity.* Grand Rapids, MI/Cambridge: Eerdmans.

Tracy, D. (1975) *Blessed Rage for Order.* Minneapolis: Seabury Press.

SUBJECT INDEX

AUTHOR INDEX